To Ric

Glad God has connected
our paths & excited
for what He has in store!

I hope you enjoy & are
encouraged by the read.

Keep Striving,

From Here to There: A Quarter-Life Perspective on the Path to Mastery

Thane Marcus Ringler

Cover Design by **Josiah Zimmerman**

Interior Design by **Printopya**

Produced by **Thane Marcus Ringler**

ThaneMarcus.com

ISBN: 978-1-947165-93-9

Printed in the United States of America.

DEFINITIONS

"Wisdom"—Thane's definition from aggregated sources

"Mastery"—

    Definition #1—Oxford Dictionaries

    Definition #2 & #3—Merriam Webster

"Education"—

    Definition #1—Oxford Pocket English Dictionary

    Definition #2—Dictionary.com

"Learning"—Oxford Pocket English Dictionary

"Pride"—Oxford Pocket English Dictionary

"System"—Oxford Dictionaries

"Success"—Oxford Dictionaries

"Process"—Oxford Dictionaries

To the incredible team of investors behind Thane Ringler Golf: without your generosity, belief, and support, this book would never have come into being.

CONTENTS

The man who views the world at fifty the same as he did at twenty has wasted thirty years of his life.

—Muhammad Ali

INTRODUCTION

MEET THANE RINGLER

My career as a professional golfer began like a fairytale. I was starting a road trip back to my childhood home and a college buddy agreed to caddy for me in the qualifier on the way. As any good fairy tale goes, there was early turmoil—not playing well out of the gates, my caddy not knowing what he was doing, myself feeling flustered and jaded, and the reality of qualifying beginning to resemble a slowly closing door as the round neared its close. But then, *hope*. I knew I needed some magic to happen, and magic I did. The birdie, birdie, birdie finish put me in the last qualifying spot at the event. I was now a professional golfer, and my career was destined for success.

Growing up in the center of America, I was raised on hard work and good morals. Kansas was my world and adventure was my playground. I started out as a shy kid but quickly shifted to the other end of the spectrum, reinventing myself as the social butterfly I am today. I love people and believe that they deserve to be held in highest value out of all God's creation.

Yes, I did say God in the second paragraph. One thing to know about me is that I have placed my faith in Jesus Christ as my Savior, which makes me a Christian. Just as atheists cannot remove their unbelief in a god from their writing, so too I cannot separate my belief in God from what I share in this book. It is the worldview from which I see the world, and to do otherwise would be disingenuous and dishonest.

But who am I? And why does this book deserve to be read?

Usually, it boils down to snap judgments on several fronts: (1) a flashy cover that catches your eye, (2) a catchy title that sparks interest, (3) an author who is someone with something useful to share, and (4) information that is applicable to your current life. Ultimately, that judgment is up to you, but first you need to know a little more about me as context for what will follow.

I began playing golf when I was four years old but likely had a club in my hands even before then. Growing up, golf was one of the many sports I played and loved. Basketball, baseball (softball), tennis, ping pong, dodgeball, bike riding, you name it—I played them all. I loved anything that involved competition, particularly because my favorite thing to do was win. I was a desperate winner. In one instance, I practiced shuffling cards for several days just so I could be seen as the best card shuffler in school—*desperate*.

As I grew up, golf became the clear-cut favorite as my talent and developed skill were noticeable. I started to devote myself more fully to the sport, and began setting goals to accomplish along the way. After finishing a strong junior-golf career in Kansas, I left to play golf at The Master's University in California. This was advantageous in several ways: year-round good weather, a new pool of competitors, a coach I could learn much from, and a new environment to experience life in.

College continued to provide visible signs of improvement, gaining momentum and experience as the years passed. As graduation crept closer, the end goal became increasingly clear: the pursuit of a professional golf career. Almost every athlete who competes on a collegiate level will consider playing professionally, post-college. Out of that pool of athletes, only 10 percent (personal approximation) will take the thought seriously, and only 5 percent will follow through with actually giving it a shot. Upon entering the professional ranks, only 5 percent of professional athletes will be considered successful, and only 1 percent will actually be known by a majority of the audience/fans. To boil it all down, if 1 percent of all athletes end up competing professionally, then 1 percent of that pool of professional athletes will ever be known by the majority—lovingly known as "superstars"—*one* percent of *one* percent. This is especially true in the world of golf.

Statistically, I fell in line with the majority—in the pool of professional golfers not known by most fans, and not considered successful from a monetary standpoint. So why should you read a book written by someone who has had an unsuccessful and short-lived professional golf career? Because that's the life we all know. Reading a book from the 1 percent of the 1 percent is helpful and insightful, but reading a book from the 99 percent of the 1 percent—someone who can relate to the struggle, the grind, the toil in life—now that's practical; that's profound; that's *useful*.

I don't claim to know it all or to have some hidden wisdom that others don't. I do claim to have something to say and the ability to say it, which may provide you with a new perspective. I do claim that these ideas, these "mental models," these frameworks, will help you in your pursuit of mastery. Whether that path be found in the transition from college to career, or from one career to another, or from an old role to a new role, these ideas can help you travel down the path more *efficiently* and *effectively*. At least they did for me.

The last three years of playing golf professionally can best be described as incessant striving. After spending the first summer getting my bearings, so to speak, I began developing and incorporating systems within all aspects of my life to help facilitate maximum growth, expedite learning, and optimize performance. There hasn't been a stone left unturned. Along the way, this became my life-pulse, for better or for worse. And many times it was the latter.

Golf is a sport, and sports are an art form. They are the combination of technical training and massed repetition, culminating in the ability to create a desired performance. In many ways, it is the opposite of what is commonly considered art. The process of creating art begins in the right side of the brain—where insight and ingenuity lie. As you go through the action of creating that artistic thing, you transition from right side to left side as you logically think through all the finishing touches needed to turn the initial idea into a final product. In sports, and specifically in golf, you begin with a left brain, logic-forward mindset that breaks down all the components of the swing to the specific pieces needed to hit the ball from point A to point B. After much technical thought and practice have been accumulated, the performance of playing in competition requires the use of your right brain to create the end product: an artistic masterpiece—your competitive performance.

While I have become an expert in the first part of the process, I am still developing in my ability to bring out my highest ability when it matters most. This is the left-brain, free-flowing, flow-state performance that characterizes the best athletes in any sport. It is known as "being in the zone," a place where time slows down, heart-rate decreases, focus is amplified, and a relaxed confidence is produced. This is the secret sauce that produces incredible and awe-inspiring performances, loved and cherished by fans and fellow competitors alike.

In regards to this book, there is one tension that deserves mentioning. If life were a marathon (26.2 miles), I would be on mile 8. As my grandpa wisely observed, writing from a 25-year-old's perspective is dangerous. There is no possible way for me to have the knowledge, experience, or wisdom of an 80-year-old. And this is because there is no substitute for life experience—the learning from living that takes place over a lifetime of life. Telling seasoned marathoners what I believe to be true when I still haven't even reached the half-way point doesn't make any sense.

My heart in this book is not to make truth-claims about revelatory life principles for you to follow. My goal is to share the story of what professional golf has taught me in the past three-plus years, and for that narrative to provide you some measure of benefit in how you approach each stage in life, striving for excellence in what lies before you.

This is me and these are my claims.

But I challenge you to challenge me. Don't take my word for it; make me prove it. Read this book (and every book!) in a critical way. Test the things I say. Hold them to the fire and see what remains. I believe that what you will find can help—not with profound wisdom, but in practical, life-on-life ideas that fill in the gaps between where you currently are and where you want to be. I pray that it serves as the needed kick in the pants for you to **take ownership** of your life and your decisions and to **never settle** for anything less than your full potential in what you are called to in this life.

Time to get after it. Enjoy the ride.

PREFACE

WHAT THE BOOK IS ABOUT

The initial goal for this book was to write about how golf teaches you about life, and how it makes you a better person in life. Throughout the process of writing, it became clear that this wasn't what was needed to be told; it wasn't the content found deep in my soul. What unfolded over the six months of writing the initial draft was both incredible personal growth and a major shift in life.

There are two resounding themes this book represents: (1) the path of mastery, and (2) transitions in life.

Both of these themes were represented in my own life journey, from the lifelong pursuit of golf, and then in the ensuing transition from golf into new career endeavors. While these themes have distinct differences, they both revolve around the underlying theme of development, and more specifically, personal development.

Personal development is really what's at the heart of the phrase "from here to there." Figuring out how to move from here and how to get to there is something that can only be done in two ways: (1) having someone else tell/show us how to do it, or (2) figuring it out on our own. The best route is to use both options in order to get to there fastest. It is a constant, lifelong process, because once you get to there, there will always be a further there to reach.

WHAT THE PATH LOOKS LIKE

There is more to come on the concept of "mastery" itself, but it will be helpful to gain an understanding of the flow of the development process. One of the most powerful equations for the pursuit of personal development, the path of mastery, is a simple threefold process:

1. Simplicity —> 2. Complexity —> 3. Simplicity

The structure of this book follows a parallel flow. As we move from simplicity into complexity and eventually back into simplicity in the the path of mastery, so too are we going to move through the same pattern with the concepts presented in this book.

Chapters 1 to 3 (Mastery, Commitment, and Learning) make up the first stage of simplicity—the core concepts that form the foundation from which the rest of the structure is built.

Chapters 4 to 6a (Teachability, Fear, and Systems) form the ideas within the complexity stage—where the layers of information and complexity are added, and the sifting and discerning begin to take priority.

Chapters 6b to 9 (Systems, Momentum, Failure, Perspective) create the second stage of simplicity—the beginnings of simplifying all the information into what's of utmost importance and the application for the situation or circumstance at hand.

LAYOUT OF THE BOOK

While the major motifs are seen in the overall flow of mastery and the individual topics covered in that path, within each chapter I have divided the sections into three parts: (1) My Story, (2) Concept, and (3) Application. This structure is meant to provide the reader with a real-life example of what I am sharing, a clear understanding of the concept presented, and some practical ideas about how to incorporate it into life.

The reason for providing general themes for each chapter is to help you use this book as a future resource, to be able to return to the sections within each category to revisit the ideas provided for application. This is that dual responsibility of personal development—using the tools and advice given by others while taking ownership of your own life and the proper use of the information given.

THE END GOAL

The end goal is twofold. First, I want to provide insight into this process from the personal experiences I've had and the lessons I've learned along the way. Second, I want to offer practical ideas for implementing these concepts into your life in a meaningful and helpful way.

Without application, these ideas will forever remain words on a page. Without insight, they will never be seen with the childlike eyes that produce real vision, real learning, real understanding.

My encouragement to you is to use it as a resource, as a reference, as a guide. Each chapter provides its own mental model for thinking through important frameworks within the path to mastery.

1. Mastery
2. Commitment
3. Learning
4. Teachability
5. Fear
6. Systems
7. Momentum
8. Failure
9. Perspective

As you move through the words ahead, be sure to take stock of where you are in the path and what the context is within the big picture of the entire journey—not just the path of mastery and the road of self-development, but also the process of life. Use this book as a tool, as a resource, as a guide, but application is only as useful as its context. Right application in the wrong context = wrong application. Read this book in light of where you are in life, and use it accordingly.

Let's begin, shall we?

Phase One: Simplicity

MASTERY

"If people knew how hard I had to work to gain my mastery, it would not seem so wonderful at all."

−MICHELANGELO

MY STORY

CROSSROADS MOMENTS

I began my golf career when I was four. At that time, I saw the fame, glory, and dollar signs awaiting those who gained status on the PGA Tour. I knew that I could eventually get there; it was just a matter of persistence and time. Confidence was never a problem for my four-year-old self. The game was simple: see ball, hit ball (and sometimes miss ball). For me, this was not a delusional pursuit. There were many adults telling me that I had a natural swing and a real knack for the game. In my mind, the only question that remained was, when would I finally break through?

Do you believe me?

I wouldn't, and no one should, because at four years of age I was barely conscious of life itself. What concerns us at four is chiefly learning about the new things daily life throws our way and being fed when we're hungry. That's about it. I never picked up a golf club thinking that this was my destiny. It was more akin to the new shiny object that caught my eye, sparking interest when the sun rays danced off its steel shaft. If I had to guess (and it is a guess since my memory fails me), I would say I picked up golf solely because my dad played it, which made it an obviously fun thing to do at that age.

There comes a point in life when the cliches start to sink in and the rubber meets the road. This is when you decide what life will be, what opportunities you will pursue, what habits you will form, and whether you will lead or follow. These crossroads moments are the door-frame that your life hinges on. The question is, are you going to walk through to see what's on the other side?

The point is this: four-year-olds don't set out on the path of greatness, but 24-year-olds may.

Just as I didn't set out to become a professional golfer when I picked up my first golf club at age four, so too I didn't set out to become a writer when I began my professional golf career at age 22. This highlights the reality that rarely do we make the conscious decision to arrive at where we end up. That's not to say that goals aren't important; it's more to say that the future is uncertain. With uncertainty, there is one component that has the largest effect on our ability to cope—information.

NEED TO BE INFORMED

Information is empowering. With it, change is possible. Without it, despair is probable. Full information is rarely available, but having even partial information may be all that's needed.

Rarely do we recognize the value of information—until it is taken away, that is. I recently traveled through an international airport (that will go unnamed) when I was met head-on with this reality: of all the mornings for the TSA to go on strike, it had to be the morning of my flight. Already running behind, I knew I would be cutting it close to make it through the many check-ins and security points standing between me and my gate. With stress levels already heightened above normal, I speed-walked my way toward customs. That was when I saw the line.

Typically, there are Duty-Free (aka tax-free) stores situated well before customs, in order to allow all the travelers to fulfill their retail therapy before returning home from their travels. I immediately knew something wasn't right when a line of people mysteriously appeared in the middle of the Duty-Free zone. I thought to myself, *Surely this isn't a line I have to join. Surely it's for some random gate with a large flight attached to it.* But, as I continued walking farther, it became more and more apparent that there was very little chance I would escape this monstrous queue.

Thankfully, there were several airport attendants (and some workers from the various airlines) who were near the front of the line directing traffic and informing all the bewildered travelers why there was such a massive line and why they had to go back and stand in it. Without these attendants explaining the situation things would have deteriorated rapidly; even with their help there was no shortage of yelling and cursing, with dozens of passengers steadily moving closer to hysteria and rage.

While the story ended like every great superhero movie (good guy wins, bad guy loses)—with the flights waiting until their passengers made it through the gate before taking off—it left a lasting impression on me about the power of information, *especially* on a large scale. But its power isn't reserved for only the group level; it is just as important on an individual level if success is to follow.

PURPOSE OF THIS CHAPTER

The purpose of this chapter (and this book as a whole) is to share information. Living informed is always a better alternative to a life of ignorance. Making informed decisions always trumps stumbling blindly down life's path.

> "Smart people learn from their mistakes. Wise people learn from the mistakes of others."

While information can't fully replace the power of personal experience, it will help guide us down our journey for a smoother ride.

This relates to how I think about wisdom. Wisdom is defined simplistically as: "the proper application of knowledge." In my current place in life, the path of growing in wisdom involves accumulating both *knowledge* and *experience*. Neither part can be replaced or removed. There are no cheat codes to circumvent their necessity. While there is more to defining the full scope of wisdom (discernment, judgment, circumspection, etc.), knowledge plus experience is a good place to start.

Mastery is a sub-type of wisdom. It is the application of wisdom acquired, in a specific field or skill, that enables your highest potential output, and exceeds the ability of the majority in that field. Mastery is a quest, a journey that takes patience, persistence, and practice.

This concept is best summarized by Peter Brown: "Mastery, especially of complex ideas, skills, and processes, is a quest. It is not a grade on a test, something bestowed by a coach, or a quality that simply seeps into your being with old age and gray hair."

Point being, mastery doesn't happen by chance.

CONCEPT

WHY

Knowing what mastery is—what it looks like and what it entails—is necessary and important. But information is merely that—information. Knowing doesn't equate to believing. There is some power in knowing; there is *great* power in believing. We must *believe* that the pursuit of mastery is a worthy endeavor, *and* we must understand why.

Why should you pursue mastery? Why push for excellence? Why work toward being the best you can be? Why does it matter?

We all fall in different places on the spectrum from idealism to cynicism. I've been blessed with a healthier than normal dose of idealism, and I wish the same was true for everyone. Idealism helps us understand why the pursuit of mastery is important, because the pursuit of mastery is an idealistic endeavor. It's pushing beyond our current reality to what lies beyond our grasp. It's believing we can accomplish the impossible, or at least the improbable. It's tackling the daunting task despite the odds of failing being high.

But why?

Because human and societal progress *depends* on it. Progress is up to *you*.

Life is not meaningless. As a Christian, I believe life has *eternal* value not just for us but in God's eyes. Regardless of your faith, life is endowed with meaning from our ability to love and care for each other. Helping those in need fills our hearts with joy and gives our lives meaning that will never be achieved through self-centered goals or pursuits.

The world we live in is filled with problems yearning for solutions. It's not hard to see. In fact, it would be incredibly hard to miss! Every day we are faced with real-life examples of these problems waiting for answers. Solutions are never handed to us; they are *always* fought for.

Mastery matters because people matter, because *you* matter. Pursuing your highest skill, knowledge, ability, etc.—*that* is what will lead to growth, first on an individual level and then on a collective societal level. It always starts with you.

> *"Be the change that you wish to see in the world."*
> —Mahatma Gandhi

Mastery matters.

DEFINE TERMS

Okay, so, what is mastery? What is *true* mastery? How does one achieve it? Is it achievable?

These questions have been asked and pursued for as long as competitive sports or competitive careers have been around. There is no shortage of books, videos, online forums, conferences, and think-tanks mining the depths of how you develop superior skill.

From the view of a dictionary, "mastery" is defined as "comprehensive knowledge or skill in a subject or accomplishment"; "possession or display of great skill or technique"; "skill or knowledge that makes one master of a subject." Beyond simply defining terms, one of the best ways to understand something so lofty is by looking to those who have illustrated its beauty for us.

Frederic Chopin is considered to be Poland's greatest composer. Mastery is unquestionably attributed to his skill and works. Here's what he had to say about mastery: "Simplicity is the final achievement. After one has played a vast quantity of notes and more notes, it is simplicity that emerges as the crowning reward of art."

Before discussing his observation, it is important to mention that human capacities vary. Chopin's level of natural skill, talent, and proficiency does not equal mine, nor does it equal yours. Each individual person has *individual* strengths and weaknesses. Each person has been given greater or lesser opportunity than someone else. The point isn't in the final level of mastery; it is to reach *your* level of mastery.

While it is possible to find a standard that's accepted by the majority, it is far more helpful to think about mastery on a different level. Mastery should be (and can be) an *individualized* pursuit. And that is why beginning with the end in mind is so important. Choosing a path that is aligned with your predisposed strengths and talents is a wise path to take.

SYNONYMS

Back to Chopin.

Within his words, mastery was not present in form, but rather in spirit. Chopin states that "simplicity is the final achievement." He's saying that the final achievement from the pursuit of excellence is … simplicity?

A few years ago I heard a phrase for the first time: "simplicity on the far side of complexity." It was a thought-provoking phrase and it revealed a lot about the process of proficiency. After sitting with the phrase, I began to realize several things. The first thing I realized was the underlying assumption present in the phrase. If the point is to look at the far side of complexity, then the assumption is that we already know what's on the near side. It quickly became clear that simplicity is both the treasure found on the far side of complexity and the foundation upon which that complexity is built.

The second observation that stemmed from the phrase was that this is an extreme *oversimplification* of the journey to mastery—which is the point. An idea, task, or skill is one of two options: (1) simple, or (2) complex. So if simplicity is what creates the foundation for complexity, how can it also be found on the far side of that same complexity?

Mastery, like wisdom, is the proper application of the amassed skill or knowledge you have in any given subject or field. It comes from having learned the foundational elements—the simple building blocks in the early stages of new learning—then wading through the depths of complexities, amassing more and more information and accumulating layers upon layers of skills, ideas, and concepts, all before becoming a master of said subject or skill—meaning, you are able to know which one small detail out of the ocean of possibilities is *most* important and *most* applicable to the specific situation or scenario in front of you. The simplest solutions to the most complex problems—that is mastery; that is simplicity on the far side of complexity.

One glaring example is the device held in the hands of a majority of Americans today: the iPhone. Apple is a brand built on simplicity. From product design, to branding and advertisement, to functionality and user interface, it all screams simplicity.

This is not by mistake.

The late, renowned co-founder of Apple, Steve Jobs, stated, "Simple can be harder than complex: You have to work hard to get your thinking clean to make it simple. But it's worth it in the end because once you get there, you can move mountains."

And that he did, creating a legacy that continues to thrive even in his absence. In the midst of a rapidly advancing field of complexities, simplicity still triumphs over all.

EQUATION REVISITED

Simplicity —> Complexity —> Simplicity

An easy way to visualize this process is within the categories of Beginner, Intermediate, and Advanced. To help illustrate the path, I am going to use golf as an example (but any skill or job can work).

Simplicity—Beginner

This is starting from ground zero. You are coming to a topic, an endeavor, an occupation, a career, or a hobby with very little understanding of the working parts involved. You go to the driving range with a bag of weird-looking sticks and start trying to hit a tiny white ball. (Hopefully there's a little more context, but you get the point.)

This is the phase when you are learning the fundamentals of the activity itself—from laying the foundation for motor-memory within the body, to experiencing all the different facets of each skill and component, to learning about the different tools and the situations when you use them.

In golf, this begins with learning how to hold the club, how to stand in relation to the ball, what the swing should look like, what the swing feels like, what to focus on, what each club should do, etc. In this stage, the best advice is the simplest advice: "Keep your head down." "Keep your eyes on the ball." "Don't swing out of your shoes." "Rotate with your body."

As you progress though this stage, you move from being a complete novice to feeling more like a regular member of that broader community (in this example, as a golfer). The focus for this phase is largely repetition-based (the more reps the better) to train the body in what it needs to do and to gain the level of skill needed to be a consistent producer and competitor within the space you reside.

Complexity—Intermediate (and Advanced)

As your experience grows, you will start to recognize which areas of your toolkit (skill set) are stronger or weaker than others. You will begin to ingrain, both mentally and physically, the over-arching principles for success that are widely preached and accepted by your field at large. Some common examples of this in golf are: "par is a good score," "play to your strengths," "be patient," "drive for show; putt for dough," etc.

Building good habits is a must, and as you gain confidence and aptitude, pressure will start to be applied through competition, deadlines, expectations, and responsibilities. This pressure refines your understanding of where your skill level really lies, enabling you to further refine your skills, knowledge, and habits for further development. Being taught by a mentor, senior co-worker, or coach is also very important in this phase, as you continue adding layers of knowledge to your base foundation.

This step is by far the largest in terms of scope and the longest in terms of duration. In any field, career, or sport (and especially in golf), as you dive deeper, there can be an endless depth to its facets and complexities. The more you know, the more you begin to realize how much you don't know. After I had finished my first year of college, I honestly couldn't fathom how I had ever played golf as a junior not knowing what I now knew. And again, the same experience took place after my first year of playing professionally. The layers build and build upon each other until there is a mountain of experience and knowledge to pull from.

Simplicity—Expert

This phase of simplicity is greatly desired but rarely acquired. As Steve Jobs stated, it takes a lot of knowledge and skill to cut through the crap and distill the gold of simplicity in the midst of an informational tsunami. When you build a mountain's worth of information, experience, skill, and knowledge, finding that one piece that you need becomes a much more difficult task. The needle in the haystack is only as difficult as the size of the haystack.

Characteristics of this stage include the establishment of mental models (a framework) to operate off of, a deep familiarity with personal mannerisms and your internal wiring, the ability and discipline to *not* be confused or overcome by complexities, confidence without ignorance (*very* difficult to accomplish), keen discernment of the core principles underlying various concepts, and an awareness of (and focus on) remedying root causes, not merely their symptoms.

In golf, this looks like becoming a master of your mind, discovering and committing to the best system *for your game*, being comfortable in every environment, dictating your emotions instead of the other way around, doing the fundamentals extremely well, having enough experience to know what each situation and circumstance leads to and what type of shot to hit as a result (and not only knowing but also *believing* that intuition), and on and on.

The point to understand with this phase is that it takes a long time to get there; and usually when you think you've finally arrived, you've only just begun.

"There will come a time when you believe everything is finished. That will be the beginning."
—Louis L'Amour

THE IMPORTANCE OF ROAD MAPS

I remember the first time I came to L.A. Moving from a small town in Kansas to one of the largest metropolitan city centers in the world is undoubtedly daunting. Fortunately, I was blessed with perfect timing. The year I moved—2010—was the year I got my first smartphone, and with it a personal, portable GPS. What a savior! Road maps are *essential* to getting where you need to go in the least amount of time possible. Road maps lead to efficiency.

This is similar with books. Every book shares similar characteristics: a title, a summary on the back or on the cover, a table of contents, maybe even an intro *and* a preface (guilty). In order for us to be motivated to read a book, we need to have a base understanding of what it's about. Without a road map, reading a book would be a complete guessing game. We can always improve our discernment of which books are helpful to read and which are a waste of time, but that takes accumulated experience and involves much more than a simple back-cover analysis. Moral of the story: road maps make a difference.

This chapter is about road maps, while the rest of the book is more focused on the best practices/mental models to use once the quest has begun. But not only road maps, this chapter is about goal setting—beginning with the end in mind, starting with why, living a purpose-driven life. It doesn't matter how you say it; the truth remains. If we are going to be successful, then we have to know what that means, not just theoretically, but also personally. It doesn't matter what that means to your mom, your neighbor, your boss, your best friend, or your role model. It matters what that means to *you*. And because it matters, it needs to be defined—personally.

Beyond personal meaning, the path doesn't have to be paved anew every time it's traveled on. Those who came before have traversed this road already, which allows those who follow to have an already-established path to take. There's no need to reinvent the wheel at the turn of every century. At the end of the day, a wheel is a wheel, and down the road it rolls.

There is so much to this concept, which makes it difficult to distill into a digestible form. And that itself is an important indicator *of* mastery: can you understand a concept fully enough to hold an intelligent conversation with other experts in the field while also maintaining the ability to explain it so that a six-year-old can understand?

"If you can't explain it to a six year old, you don't understand it yourself."
—Albert Einstein

This is that six-year-old version of the road map:

Simplicity —> Complexity —> Simplicity.

So, while mastery is the implicit focus of this book, it is the explicit purpose of this chapter. Understanding what mastery is, what it entails, and why it's worth pursuing is vital to living life well. It is a nonnegotiable in becoming your best for the world's greatest good.

With this, the order is important. There are five reasons why beginning with an understanding of the road map is crucial for success in your quest:

- If you don't know where you're going, then you will never get there (purpose).

- If you don't know how you will get there, then you'll never arrive (preparation).

- If you don't know the order of steps to get there, then you will waste precious time running circles around yourself (process).

- If you don't understand the approximate length of the trip, then you'll never reach your destination (patience).

- If you don't have an awareness of the inherent obstacles, then you won't have the tenacity to overcome them (persistence).

Before getting to the practical application of these five signposts needed for any journey, we need to take a look at one of our greatest weaknesses: the longing for *shortcuts*.

SHORTCUTS

In modern society, get-rich-quick schemes are all the rave. They have been rebranded in many different forms, including the infamous fill-in-the-blank hackers (life hackers, bio-hackers, growth hackers, etc.). If anyone is a big fan of these trends, it would be me. I always love a good shortcut to success; and if it works, then what's the harm?

At the root of this inner tendency is a war waged between short-term gain and. delayed gratification. On one side, shortcuts lead to eating the cookie sooner—fulfilling the desire that begins welling within our tastebuds the moment we smell them coming out of the oven. On the other hand, delaying that impulse allows us to say no to something that is so, so good in the moment yet produces unwanted results in the future (taken to the extreme: diabetes, obesity, etc.).

One of the biggest dangers with the shortcut mindset is the way we begin to train ourselves to think. It is forming the habit, the discipline, of giving into our impulsive desires, which is not as dependent on whether the desire itself is helpful or hurtful. The other problem that comes from shortcuts is the rebranding of success. Success begins to turn into getting to X, Y, or Z faster than anyone else, no matter the cost. Burning bridges is rarely the answer.

A quote my grandpa shared helps clarify this: "Success is a road, not a destination."

Shortcuts, success hacks, alternative paths: all can be a good thing, and, on their face, these mindsets are a good thing. But success does *not* equal mastery. Arriving at a destination only means that it's time to either (a) get to work with where you are now at, or (b) pick a new destination to push toward.

When we zoom out to a broader perspective, sustained success occurs when simplicity is achieved on the far side of complexity. Sure, Steve Jobs could have settled for a company that solely strived to produce a percentage increase of revenues each fiscal quarter. But instead, he remained incessantly and unwaveringly committed to the best possible product, above and beyond the call of duty, all for the prize of elegant simplicity.

So, while there are no true shortcuts (or at least shortcuts that deliver on what they promise), that doesn't mean the length of your travel will be the same as your co-worker, your competitor, or your friend. The point is, the path, at its core, remains the same, but the amount of time it takes to travel down that path is up to you. The purpose of this chapter is to help you travel down that path just a little faster by gaining an understanding of the purpose, preparation, process, patience, and persistence that are *all* job requirements for the road we are on: the road of success, the road to mastery.

APPLICATION

WHY APPLY

The purpose of this book is not merely to share information but also to properly apply the ideas presented. Why apply? Because without application, information is useless. Just as our bodies need to process the food we eat in order to turn it into fuel and then discard the waste, so too our minds need to process the information we consume in order to turn it into action for the service of our world and those around us.

By discovering what the quest for mastery looks like, the goal should be to use that information to inform and assist our decisions on a weekly, monthly, and yearly basis. Our perspectives are shaped by the ideas we're taught and the events we experience throughout our lives. Now that you have a base understanding of mastery as a concept, how does this idea inform your current perspective and your future direction? Hopefully it provides an awareness for which stage of the journey you are in and patience for the process of development that always takes longer than you want.

But just because you have the right information doesn't mean you will know the right application. This is why in each chapter my aim is to provide you with a list of practical ways to apply the concepts given as suggestions for ways to put the information into action.

Even still, there are many times we face or experience anxiety from an inward lack of clarity. This is amplified by the image portrayed in others and their seeming put-togetherness.

So why do you feel hopelessly lost and forever behind all your peers who seem to have their life's plan plotted out with bullet-points, shiny resumes, vast networks/connections, and sparkling teeth to boot? The fact is, we are all in that place of anxious unknowns when transitioning from one stage of life to the next or from one stage of mastery to another. Yet that doesn't mean we have to suffer along the way. Our goal should be to thrive *regardless* of the situation, circumstance, or stage of life we're in.

To help us thrive, let's take a further look at the Five *P*s in the path to mastery.

THE FIVE P'S OF MASTERY

1. *Purpose* is the foundation of all foundations.

This is the concrete that, once poured, will forever remain as the base upon which you build your house. You may need some remodeling, or maybe even a complete demolition and reconstruction, but whatever the case is, that concrete foundation will remain. Even if you happened to move to a new city with a new home and a new life and a new you, the process still must begin by pouring the concrete and solidifying the rock on which you stand.

As a Christian, the underlying foundation for all I do is the hope I have in Jesus Christ and the faith I've placed in Him alone. As a result, my life is built on Him as my rock, and all I do is for the base purpose of glorifying God. What that purpose is for you may be drastically different, or similar, or maybe even the same. It is important that you clarify what your specific purpose is. If you build your house on a foundation of sandy soil, then it's liable to be compromised the instant any storm comes your way—and the storms *will* come.

We need reminders, whether it be for items from the grocery store, or the infamous to-do list, or for your grandma's birthday because you should really give her a call and sing. With how distracting life is, reminders help us elevate above the noise of everyday life to make sure we accomplish the priorities. *The* ultimate priority in beginning our journey toward mastery is our foundational why, and we need, no, we *must* remind ourselves of that foundation. Life will never automatically attach itself to our purpose.

It is often said that success doesn't happen by chance. As the writer James Clear stated, "Inspiration only reveals itself after perspiration. Optimal lives are designed, not discovered." Due to the entropy in life, stagnancy leads to decay. If we aren't moving forward, then we *will* be moving backward. If we aren't strengthening our identity through reminders of our purpose, then we will be drifting further and further away from the anchor that holds us steady. The waves of life (aka momentum) are constantly moving and disturbing our ship, bringing us up and down through the peaks and valleys, pulling us away from the path we've set to sail.

There are a handful of things we do everyday that keep us alive. Breathing, drinking water, eating food, and sleeping are the normal requirements within our everyday lives. While there are basic hygiene practices and other rituals important to functioning as a twenty-first-century human, the daily foundation of our life itself includes those four fundamental pieces: oxygen, hydration, nutrition, and rest/rejuvenation.

After reading this chapter, you need to add a fifth: the daily practice of *purpose-setting*. Just as with goals, setting your purpose at the beginning and the end of each day will enable your daily work and activities to always remain anchored to your why. This is as much of a non-negotiable to the path of mastery as water is to life. Water is essential to survive; purpose-setting is essential to thrive. Simply put, we *need* it.

Begin each day by aligning yourself with your ultimate purpose, setting it as the umbrella under which all your work resides.

2. *Preparation* ensures a better trip.

From professional athletes to business executives to store managers to culinary chefs to creatives to collegiate students and beyond—all can understand the benefit and need for proper preparation.

When taking a road trip, there is always a mental check-list to run through. Money? Check. Gas? Check. Snacks? Check. Water bottles? Check. Clothes? Check. Weather Report? Check. Miscellaneous items? Check. Directions? Check. If we don't go through this process, then it's almost guaranteed we'll end up forgetting something—ruining or, at the very least, drastically altering the entire trip altogether.

In the journey of mastery, we need to be prepared for each stage of the process. Having an understanding and awareness of the steps and cycles we'll face helps us recognize where we currently are and what we specifically need to work toward in the next phase of the process.

The esteemed Greek poet Archilochus aptly stated, "We don't rise to the level of our expectations; we fall to the level of our training."

Make sure the journey forward isn't wasted. Be well prepared and aptly trained so that you can make the road ahead count.

3. *Process* is that series of steps needed to reach your goal.

An old adage says that "two lefts don't make a right, but three do." If all you know is that you need to take a few left turns, then you could end up driving in circles, never reaching your final destination.

Seeing a birds-eye view of the general process needed to reach our goals can be a game changer. The thing to remember is that this view is just that—a *general* image of the process, not a specific snapshot. The actual steps, actions, and skills needed to reach *your* goal are going to look much different from my own as a professional golfer. The general theme is the same, but the specifics will differ.

Clarify the direction, understand the steps, trust the process.

4. *Patience* is never easy.

… especially when it comes to chocolate-chip cookies. Imagine being a four-year-old child and being given the option of having a cookie now, or waiting twenty minutes and receiving two cookies. What would you do?

Over 40 years ago, psychologist Walter Mischel of Stanford University and his colleagues conducted a study (called the Stanford Marshmallow Experiment—https://www.livescience.com/15821-cookie-test-control.html) with over 600 four-year-olds on whether they could resist the temptation of a marshmallow for 15 minutes in order to get two of them instead of just one. The results showed that only one-third of the children were able to delay gratification long enough to get the second marshmallow.

Since we have the benefit of being both older and wiser than four-year-olds, shouldn't we have better results? Theoretically, yes, but when we examine our social media usage, or our sugar intake, or how much water we drink vs. soda, alcohol, or coffee, then the results are often more dismal than we would like to admit. Just because we *should* know better, doesn't mean that we do.

Patience is never easy, but knowing how you will benefit in the long-term will help you delay gratification in the short-term.

How does this relate to the path of mastery?

Seeing and understanding the 10,000-foot view of the path ahead helps us understand that patience is needed to reach our final destination. Mastery is a long and arduous journey. Without patience, it's a journey that will quickly be forfeited or forgotten.

Patience is all about perspective. This will be a theme throughout this book. It is needed in every aspect of this journey and in every aspect of life.

5. *Persistence* is always required—no guts, no glory.

If anyone understood this truth, it would have been Winston Churchill, who is known for his outsized role in providing a unifying and motivating voice that Britain so desperately needed to withstand the war-machine of Nazi Germany during WWII. As one of the world's most prominent and cherished historical figures, he had this to say about the merit of persistence: "Continuous effort, not strength or intelligence, is the key to unlocking our full potential."

I love the word "tenacity." It carries with it such a feeling of grit from the sound and verbal structure of it. "Tenacity." This is precisely what Sir Winston is talking about—the tenacious spirit that never stops pushing the boundaries of what we believe to be personally possible.

There is not a human on this planet who wouldn't want to be described as a tenacious person—doggedly determined and resolute, both in their work and in their life. Words are easy to share, but titles—those must be earned through the institution of hard work. Hard work does not mean one day, or one week, but multiple weeks, months, and years—the kind of hard work that *persists*.

Persistence is not for the faint of heart.

IMPORTANCE OF THE BIG PICTURE

How does the overview of the path to mastery relate to the big picture of life?

Think back on your own life. Remember that time when you spent several weeks, or months, or maybe years, away from any type of weekly exercise or physical training. (Yes, we have *all* had those periods in our life. Laziness is a global malady.) In the back of your mind, you know the ship needs to be righted. Slowly but surely you build up the inner resolve and, after multiple failed attempts, craft a way to trick yourself into entering the gym and getting your sweat on.

How did that end up? *Horribly.*

The feeling can be described as "incentivizing an early death." Everything about it was awful—from your diminished athletic capacity, to your apparent and inadequate level of endurance, to your ghastly hue revealing how close you came to "lights-out." And that's just *during* the workout. But it doesn't end there. For the rest of your evening, all your energy goes to deciding if the desire to eat food outweighs your desire to raise your limp and lethargic body off the floor where you lie.

Then comes the day after. You know exactly what I mean—lactic acid for days.

This can be a traumatizing ordeal for anyone (and everyone). But tenacity is the cure—and not just any tenacity, but an *informed* tenacity.

We all have certain capacities and propensities. Some have a higher natural ability to muster up inner strength: to do what they don't want to do but know that they need to do. Others don't have that drive. Whether you have it or not, knowing the path and the associated battles that will inevitably come provides needed and welcomed assistance.

That feeling you experience during/after that first workout back never goes away. But our preparation for the impending hardship will improve with experience. The more we encounter the "suffer-fest" of a virgin workout, the better we become at aligning our expectations with the reality we will shortly face.

This pre-awareness is a game changer. Knowing that it will be grueling, draining, and seemingly unbearable allows us to prepare the "inner troops" of resolve, grit, and obstinate determination to be prepared for the onslaught ahead.

The path of mastery is no walk in the park. Anything worthwhile is hard to get. As the apostle Peter wrote in the Bible, we must "gird up our loins" and prepare to fight the good fight.

If we go into this journey with the expectation of achieving it within a calendar year, then we expose the immaturity of both our understanding and our experience. Bill Gates, a living example of mastery, poignantly said, "Most people overestimate what they can do in one year, and underestimate what they can do in ten." (Insert: lack of purpose, preparation, process, patience, and persistence.)

This is not a mastery hack. This is a road map to where you are heading, giving you both the directions of how to get there and an increased awareness of what the path will entail: both the good, the bad, and the ugly—because they will all be there. There are no short-cuts in life. There are just those who run the road faster *and* smarter.

This is that journey. Hope for the best, expect the worst.

Let's start running.

2

COMMITMENT

"The most difficult thing is the decision to act, the rest is merely tenacity."

—AMELIA EARHART

MY STORY

FROM COLLEGE TO CAREER

Why does commitment matter?

This was an honest question that remained unresolved for much of my first year as a professional golfer, albeit not a question I posed consciously. Lurking in my subconscious was the doubt of commitment actually being a nonnegotiable; the doubt that being sold-out is worth it; the fear that comes from the unknowns, hiding in the shadows of my adaptive unconscious.

It all started my senior year of college. I spent the summer between my junior and senior year of college wrestling with the decision of whether or not professional golf was my ultimate destiny. From time spent reflecting and introspecting, as well as the advice from individuals in my life, the decision was finally made. Professional golf was a go.

Making this decision a year in advance was important to me, because the thing I hated most was wasted time. If I was able to put in the legwork needed to raise the funds for my professional career before I graduated, then I'd be able to hit the ground running immediately after graduation. And that is exactly what I did: collaborating with my grandpa on the right business model for both "Thane (the Golfer)" and "The Investor," of whom God blessed me with an initial group of ten individuals. This was an arduous process at times, but with a year's head start I was able to have most of the structure and funds in place by the time I became a college graduate.

The type of investment I was seeking (and requesting) is not your typical type of investment. In fact, it would more accurately be defined as glorified gambling—betting on which horse will win the race. It is the type of investment that would be better classified as a "donation."

Throughout this time of fund-raising, I was pitching my plan to various men and women in my life. With the business plan I had created, and the schedule I had mapped out for the years ahead, I felt an inner tension at play. It was the tension that any and every entrepreneur faces: the tension of: confidently predicting the unpredictable - my future. The tension of selling out to a pursuit that could ultimately leave you hung out to dry.

As a result of this tension, and my naivety (youthful immaturity), there was one seemingly obscure prescription that turned out to be a pill I couldn't swallow. This was the prescription of *commitment*.

COACH JASON'S ADVICE

One of the most influential voices in my life during my collegiate years was my golf coach, Jason Semelsberger (yes, it's a mouthful). He provided countless advice and wisdom not only as a golfer, but also as a person, especially during the transitionary years from boyhood to manhood. Since he had experience playing professional golf during his own career, I relied heavily on his experience and expertise to help guide and direct my formation and direction during my post-college career.

One of the stories he shared on multiple occasions was of an interaction he had had with a friend of his who was, and still is, a successful professional golfer. Coach Jason had seen this player while practicing, and since he had started to have some success in his pro-career,

Jason asked him what had changed or sparked the success. This player responded with an almost-resentful admonition of Jason, saying that there was never a doubt he would make it. The resounding message he emphatically communicated to him was that there was simply *no other option.*

This story has stuck with me for several reasons: practically, because Coach Jason used it frequently (and for good reason!), but also because that story shares a common theme with the story of virtually every successful professional golfer on tour. When asked what they would be doing if they weren't a professional golfer, they have *no* answer.

When hearing this story during my senior year of college, I simply couldn't relate. I wasn't in a place of pure commitment. I wasn't 100 percent sold-out to the cause. My rational, pragmatic side was too loud for this truth to take hold of my heart and my mind. I could logically ascent to its benefit but not willingly submit to its belief. The wisdom I adopted was that of rational security—the belief that you must have a plan in place for when things go bad, for the possibility of failure, for the chance that you don't do what you are setting out to do. Ultimately, it is the belief of unbelief—commonly known as *doubt.*

It wasn't until I had played professionally for several years that I was able to understand this concept and accept its truthful claims. This took me two years too long; but hopefully this story (and this chapter) can help you overcome this obstacle faster and commit to commitment *now.*

CONCEPT

IT COMES WITH A PRICE

There's a very common example that illustrates this idea of commitment. With the recent conflicts America has found itself in, there isn't an American who hasn't heard about the fighting force sitting at the top of the food chain, the elite of the elite. From movies to books to memoirs and beyond, the posse, prowess, and power of these warriors are unparalleled. They truly are "the few" and "the proud" within the group that has adopted that motto. They are none other than the U.S. Navy SEALs.

While there are countless lessons to be learned from their accomplishments—cultivating such incredible and deserved notoriety—the one worth examining here is their process of initiation.

To earn the title of U.S. Navy SEAL, you must complete a six-month BUDS school and then a seven-month SEAL qualification program. There are varying numbers on what percentage of candidates make it through the program, but the consensus is that it's low—*very* low. At its core, the purpose of the SEAL instructors during the entry school and program is to persuade the candidates to quit. Through physical, mental, and verbal harassment, they succeed with a majority of their candidates.

But why? What's the purpose? Why would their goal be to make those who begin wanting to join end up wanting to leave?

By this point you should be able to guess the answer: *commitment.*

Commitment costs. It comes with a price, and that price is sacrifice—what you give up in order to be committed to what you're pursuing. In the case of the SEALs, it comes with a high physical, mental, and emotional cost; but in every level or type of commitment, it will cost you something.

True and deep commitment has lasting presence, even to the point of death. Does the phrase "till death do us part" ring a bell?

NO PLAN B

Every fight or battle has several aspects that are always present. They have both winners and losers, casualties, mistakes, lasting ramifications, and typically some transference of harm. But, at their core, every fight is founded on a *belief.*

Not only do we fight for *what* we believe, but also we fight *to* believe. And the number-one enemy we face in this fight is doubt.

My personal hesitation to commit all parts of my being, both externally and internally (the harder half), to the pursuit of golf was because I was allowing the weed of doubt to be planted alongside all the rest of the seeds of the crop I was trying to harvest. I wanted to turn a blind eye to their presence, but I knew deep down that I was trying to do all I could to get around the vulnerability of being all in.

Usually the way we get around being 100 percent sold-out is by following the logical practice of planning for contingencies. When something is contingent, it means that thing is possible or likely, but not certain to happen. Thus, a contingency plan is a plan based on the possibility that something *may* happen in the future. But the core premise of every contingency plan is that the first plan of attack—plan A—will not succeed.

So often our culture praises the "wisdom" found in having a backup plan. Contingency planning is the bee's knees. The more options the better. Plan for the worst, expect the best. Right?

If you didn't catch it, the correct phrase is actually "Plan for the best, expect the worst." This does *not* mean, make plan A but also make plan B since the worst-case scenario is that plan A fails. Rather, it's saying to plan for everything to go horribly wrong but expect plan A to work because of your ability to overcome obstacles.

We can always plan our way through hardships, but if we expect the very path we are pursuing to fail, then why are we pursuing it in the first place? At the heart of this proverb is not our need to plan for failure, yet how often do we use it as justification to do just that? This saying reveals our need to be emotionally prepared to face the obstacles and challenges always present in any journey or career.

PLAN A.5

So, what if we commit to plan A and then also come up with a secondary plan B (or plan C) that we hold in the back of our mind? What could be the harm? Besides, it helps us sleep better at night and we just feel more comfortable with having options.

To be honest, this was the true cause for my doubting of Coach Jason's advice. Not having any other options, any other contingency plans, was extremely uncomfortable for me (and seemingly unwise). But, despite what the American "prosperity gospel" preaches, comfort is *not* the goal. Comfort should be approached cautiously and critically, never flippantly, because it too comes with a cost.

A practical example of this cost can be seen through the example of our physical bodies.

The human body is amazingly adaptive. We have been created to survive in some of the harshest natural conditions, both through our mental capacities (in creating solutions and solving problems that arise) and in our bodies' programmed responses. Our bodies have been designed to effectively cope with the various dangers and stressors we inevitably encounter in life.

One example of this is our autonomic nervous system. The whole point behind the title "autonomic" is that it operates automatically without the conscious directing of the brain. The two parts of this system are (1) the sympathetic nervous system and (2) the parasympathetic nervous system. These two systems operate in tandem to allow the body to respond in accordance to the demands required in different scenarios.

If we see a tiger (imminent danger), our body will immediately activate the sympathetic nervous system (known as the state of "fight or flight") that enables our body to, in its fullest capacity, either fight the enemy or run away from the enemy. Some of the internal mechanisms include an increased heart rate, constriction of blood vessels, dilation of the eyes, and a slowing down of the digestive system—all aiding our ability to survive. Once the threat no longer exists, our parasympathetic nervous system gets to work in restoring the status quo within the body. This response includes a decreased heart rate, dilation of the pupils, increased digestion, and a relaxing of the sphincter muscles.

This finely tuned system is amazingly effective. But there's a problem: Our incessant effort to create and commercialize comfort is dampening our body's ability to adapt to changes in the environment. Along with this dampening, we are over-activating our stress response in situations when it isn't necessary—in the absence of real danger. With over-activation (aka being stressed out) comes a reduction in our body's ability to effectively balance itself out.

So, from a physiological sense, comfort is the enemy of adaptability. Heated seats, thermostat-controlled air conditioners, water heaters, lazy chairs, all-you-can-eat buffets, etc.—all contribute to diminishing some portion of our capacity to adapt. Sure, these are not bad things (most of them are really good inventions that I'm thankful for!), but when we never allow our body the opportunity to exercise adaptation, it loses the very ability *to* adapt.

This correlation is seen not just literally within our physiology but also figuratively within our headspace and our minds. Choosing the easy path, the path of comfort, produces a brittle mind that isn't able to tackle tough challenges, isn't able to resist temptation, isn't able to remain confident regardless of the external circumstances, isn't able to believe in itself when no one else does. The mind longs for comfort just as much as the body does, and there are definitely times when it can be useful for rest or recovery, but more times than not it's just our laziness kicking in. Plan A.5 is a great comfort to the mind when you start any endeavor, but comforts can be dangerous.

Why is having a plan A.5 dangerous? The answer is: *doubt*. The entrance of doubt, no matter the size, is like planting a single weed in a field of wheat. As soon as that one weed takes root, it will spread throughout the entire crop if left unchecked. If we're honest with ourselves, contingencies give us a way out of the responsibility and ownership tied to our current pursuit.

Stop giving yourself a way out, no matter how "wise" it feels, because that wisdom is largely tied to comfort, and comfort tends to stunt our growth more than foster it.

THE PATH OF COMMITMENT

Contingency planning, despite its appearance of wisdom, is not compatible with being sold out to plan A, to being *committed*.

So how do we move from contingent to committed?

A quote that was placed on the wall of a gym I used to frequent read, "If it is meant to be, it is up to me." The first step comes in the decision to take *ownership* of your beliefs, followed by the effortful discipline to validate and solidify that belief in your mind. This war to believe is waged against your number-one enemy: doubt. The voice of doubt resides in an inescapable place: within your mind. Running away from it is not an option because your mind will always be there. The path forward is not in avoiding it but in silencing it.

The fruit of this labor is found in the (realistic) confidence we produce and maintain. Realism is inherently tied to an objective reality. Growth in our own objective confidence, within what we are pursuing, takes a lot of effort and a lot of fighting. But usually the thing it requires most is *time*. Which is why being sold-out and committed is a nonnegotiable—so that you can withstand the cultural pressures, your innate propensity toward laziness and comfort, and the cracking of the door for doubt to slip into the mind and wreak havoc.

Over *time*—that all-important and inescapable tutor—competence and growth occurs. This will look like a combination of both knowledge and experience—which make up both the theoretical and practical understanding of the skill set and tools you need to successfully pursue mastery within any field.

WHAT STANDS IN OUR WAY?

"Hard work is the price of success."
—John Crowley

At the root of the obstacles blocking our path is a four-letter word: *fear*. Commitment issues always stem from a fear of failure. There are several ways this manifests:

1. Fear of Becoming Lost

Anytime you begin a voyage, you take on certain risks associated with the journey. One of those risks is taking a wrong turn, leading to a new status: *lost*. Being lost means you are unable to find your way; your current whereabouts are largely unknown. A good example of this would be trying to navigate Los Angeles in the pre-GPS era (so thankful I didn't have to face this). Becoming lost is a very real and valid fear we all face at times. Feelings of hopelessness and helplessness are what often accompany this state.

Yet there are several false assumptions underlying this fear. The first is that we knew where we were going in the first place. Sure, when you have a scheduled commitment to be in a location at a specific time, you know exactly where you *want* and *need* to be in that moment. But in life, rarely do we know *exactly* where we should be at the beginning of the voyage. Outside sources can tell us what the ideal destination is, but life is hardly ever idealistic, and adopting idealism as a personal norm is certainly not realistic.

The other false assumption is that not reaching your destination is a bad thing. Yes, the travels may not go according to plan, but that can facilitate many unforeseen opportunities—such as where you currently are as a result of your new status. When we start a trip, we have limited knowledge of what lies ahead. Thus, we can't possibly know if our planned destination is the best possible outcome. If we want to drive from Houston to Los Angeles but end up in Kansas, who's to say that isn't a better place to be?

2.   Fear of Dead-Ends

Everybody hates wasting things. Even at an all-you-can-eat buffet, deep inside we always feel bad leaving uneaten food on the plate. In any creative career, mistakes can suck the lifeblood out of you. Having to re-do work is enough to drive artists into admittance at an asylum.

Think about running the 1,600-meter race in track. You meticulously follow your pre-race routine, making sure you are well hydrated, limber, and warm enough to have good blood flow. The start time has arrived and you all step up to the line. *BANG!* Now you're running, pacing yourself so as to have enough kick in the tank to finish with a burst. Then, all of a sudden, you make that last reach over the finish line and it's over. You ran your heart out and are now anxiously awaiting your official time. But there's a problem. Someone had a false start—and now you all have to re-do the race. Talk about a real-life nightmare.

Running in vain is terrifying.

Now, obviously this would never *actually* happen, but that's the point. False starts are corrected before the race is run so that you don't have to redo the whole race.

Life isn't as predictable as a race around the track. We can't fully see if where we are moving will result in a dead end. But similar to false starts in track, dead ends in life don't mean we have to start over from scratch. We've traveled this far already, so there's no point in traveling all the way back to the start before we begin again. Pivoting well means that we are able to move slightly backward, and then start traveling in a new, *forward* direction.

Wasted opportunities are subject to the same fear as running in vain. But opportunities are never wasted unless you allow them to be. Each situation, scenario, or circumstance in life *can* be helpful to your overall journey, but only if it remains attached to your anchor—your foundational purpose underlying all that you do. If you're running the race to be the fastest runner *you* can be, then running it again will only help you by adding further experience, endurance, and mental toughness to your arsenal.

3. *Fear of Dangerous Roads*

One of my true loves in life is riding motorcycles, and more specifically, sport bikes—fondly known as "crotch rockets". Motorcycles can be scary. The majority of people have a healthy fear of them (healthy in that it is fully rational to not want to ride one on a road with other moving vehicles). But why don't we have that same fear of driving cars on those exact roads with the very same dangers as a motorcycle? The fact is, riding a motorcycle leaves you fully exposed. While the road risks are nearly identical, the brevity of consequences in the case of an accident are elevated to the extreme on motorcycles.

Rarely, if ever, do we think about the risks we assume when driving a car. This is mostly due to the nature of the world and the culture we live in. Imagine how silly it would be to turn down a job because it wasn't within *walking* distance—stemming from the fear of having to commute daily in a car on dangerous roads.

This is the same irrational logic we consider "normal" when trying to figure out what job to pursue or which career path to take. The reality is, we never know which trip down the dangerous road will result in a safe trip and which will result in an accident. The road is always dangerous, but that shouldn't hinder us from moving forward down that road.

The average performer will follow the logic that security equals success. This isn't bad logic or necessarily wrong, but it is limiting. High-performers understand that risk is the fire that refines our personal capacities and allows us to reach (and expand) our full potential.

Commitment is all about freedom—freedom from our doubts, freedom to embrace our full potential, freedom to be fully invested in the work that is before us, freedom to choose a direction and move *forward*.

APPLICATION

BECOME A STEPPER

What's true in the beginning of life holds true throughout the rest of life: the first step is always the hardest.

During the transformative stage from squirming baby blob into infancy all the way into being a toddler, every little boy or girl begins growing individual fingers and toes, and may even sprout some wispy hair on the soil of their skull. Throughout this process of development and literal growth, they begin to crawl from point A to point B and start attempting to grasp things above their lowly reach. At this stage, they begin to become fed up with the status quo of being a bottom dweller. They want to graduate to the big leagues. They want to *walk*.

So, as their loving parent, you hold them and illustrate what walking entails. You provide the "training wheels" so that they can acclimate to being vertically oriented, in greater opposition to the forces of gravity at play. This emboldens them to begin pulling themselves up against couches or chairs. The carrot dangling in front of their head is so close to being grasped they can almost taste it. Then comes the day—that first step. Hours, days, even months went into this climactic moment. And immediately after stepping forward, their legs crumble beneath them, crashing to the floor. But what a moment! What an accomplishment!

Now you are sitting here reading this book and so much has changed—but not as much as you think. The path of learning still follows a similar theme, and that first step is still the hardest one to make.

No picture of this is clearer than the period of time after graduating college.

From the time you became an upperclassmen, everyone (and their mom) predictably asks you what you want to do with your life. The underlying connotation communicated is that you need to have your whole life figured out—*now*.

But you don't. And no one does. Knowing your destiny as a student in college is as rare a feat as an 18-year-old scoring 25 points in his rookie season debut in the NBA. Chances are, you're not LeBron James.

The funny thing is, after working so hard to become a stepper as a child, we slowly digress into being a sitter in our adult lives. Being a sitter means you rest on your laurels, allowing all the progress you've made thus far succumb to the inescapable process of decay. No one sets out to be a sitter, but with age comes this natural byproduct. Yet we don't have to resign ourselves to this outcome. We all can make the conscious decision to stage a comeback, to become a stepper once again. The beauty of being a stepper is that the steps get easier the better you get at stepping. After a child's first steps are accomplished, it's not very long before she is running all over the house with her newfound confidence in a skill that took so much effort to gain one mere step in.

Commitment always starts with a step, moving forward down the path set before you. Take action; take that first step.

WHAT IT DOESN'T MEAN

It's important to have a level head about what commitment truly means, and this starts with knowing what it doesn't mean.

There are several myths we believe that keep us from being committed:

1. Commitment means that once you make a decision you can't go back. *False.*

Being sold-out to an endeavor does *not* mean you can't change paths or quit your current work that, at one point, was the best option for your path forward. The old adage goes, "You don't know until you try," and that depicts the value of experience. Usually the thing we lack most is experience, and you can't read a book to learn that. It requires the act of *doing.* So make an informed decision and commit to it.

2. When the going gets tough, it's an obvious sign you made the wrong decision. *False.*

Commitment does not only apply to the situations or times when it's easy to be committed. In fact, commitment is really all about staying the course, *especially* when the going gets tough. This is why they say, "When the going gets tough, the tough gets going."

There will be unforeseen challenges and hardships associated with every job, occupation, or career. Commitment must be sustained for a long enough span of time to get the full experience of what that path entails, as well as a deep enough understanding of yourself to make a decision that's informed from both the head and the heart (knowledge and experience). Typically, this cannot be achieved in under a year's time.

WHAT IT DOES LOOK LIKE

Commitment does not mean you have your entire life figured out. What it does mean is that after choosing the best path forward (considering your strengths, interests, and present opportunities), you begin *moving with commitment* in that direction. Walking forward on the path you've chosen requires not just commitment but also *conviction*.

Seth Godin, famous author and marketer, knew the importance of this truth, so much so that he wrote an entire book on this one principle: *The Dip*. "The Dip is the long slog between starting and mastery." Typically, it's the time when the going gets really tough and you start to consider whether you should stick it out or quit. Seth makes the case that quitting is a good option, especially if you aren't going to be the best in the world at whatever it is you're pursuing. He calls it "strategic quitting," saying that it's "the secret of successful organizations." In contrast, "reactive quitting and serial quitting are the bane of those that strive (and fail) to get what they want." (*The Dip*, pp. 16-17).

Commitment isn't easy. Seth went on to say, "If it doesn't cost you your life, it isn't a quest" (p. 25). The path to mastery, the quest you are on, is no different. Commitment takes *sacrifice*. That's why quitting and commitment go hand in hand; committing entails quitting—quitting anything that detracts you from being the best you can be at the path you are pursuing.

Quitting is also a factor for informed commitment. There's a difference between commitment that is helping and furthering your cause and commitment that's hurting your cause and your future. Seth describes this understanding well in saying, "Persistent people are able to visualize the idea of light at the end of the tunnel when others can't see it. At the same time, the smartest people are realistic about not imagining light when there isn't any" (p. 55).

Being committed is a balance. It's a balance of the eyes—erring neither on blindness (walking with our eyes closed) nor on panoramic vision (walking with a focus on all that's around us, not wanting to miss any piece or portion of it). When you walk blindly, you miss the warning signs indicating this road may not be best. Likewise, if you become overly focused on your surroundings, you will be quick to jump ship because the grass is always greener on the other side.

We must keep our eyes open with an awareness of our surroundings but with our gaze fully fixed on the road that lies ahead, the destination we are striving toward, the light at the end of the tunnel.

WHAT IT DOESN'T LOOK LIKE

There are many ways we misconstrue commitment, intentionally or not. Flat tires, chips in the windshield, running out of gas, speeding tickets, road rage—all are pitfalls we should try to avoid on any road trip.

Here are some of the pitfalls to avoid when pursuing commitment:

1. *The Pitfall of Ignorance*

Traffic signs' singular purpose is to warn motorists of what's approaching in the road ahead. Without these warnings, driving would be much more hazardous. After driving for several years, these signs become second nature to us, mainly being registered by our subconscious in the midst of our ever-wandering minds.

The same is true in life. So often there are warning signs along the path that keep us from hazardous travel. The danger comes when we miss these signs. The reason why we miss them is either because we simply don't recognize what the sign means (like when we see it for the first time) or because we ignore them. Ignorance comes in one of two forms: active or passive. Active ignorance is when we are purposefully ignoring the warning signs because we think we know best. Passive ignorance is when we ignore the warning signs simply because we aren't looking.

Commitment needs to be informed by the warning signs that appear while traveling down the road. We are all susceptible to times of ignorance. This is why we must gain objectivity from outside sources providing the balancing perspective needed to keep us from ignorance, whether passive or active.

2. The Pitfall of Elevation

Whenever the value placed on something turns ultimate, danger lurks in the distance. This truth is depicted by the phrase "absolute power corrupts absolutely." Remove the word "power" and fill in the blank with whatever it is that is "on the throne" of your heart. What is it that's ruling you, your life, your decisions, your actions, your motivations? Anytime that one thing takes ownership of your entire being—heart, soul, and mind—it will leave a path of destruction in its wake.

There are cascading effects that flow from idolatry. Blind optimism can result in ignorance of visible blind spots, which flows into willing and obstinate ignorance of anything outside of self-interest, which then begins to create casualties—both personally and relationally—and results in the burning of bridges, signifying an irreversible action from which there is no return.

Another description of this pitfall is "selling out." To sell out means to compromise your integrity, character, morality, and principles all for personal gain—which can specifically look like a lot of different things beyond mere money. The worst aspects of this pitfall are the ramifications surrounding it. More than any other pitfall, the pitfall of elevation hurts *others*. The people who are a part of your life are the ones who will bear the brunt of this burden.

The root cause for this pitfall is the loss of your why. The foundation for what you do must be regained in order to avoid catastrophic results.

3. The Pitfall of Overcommitment

More of a good thing is not always better. Excess can oftentimes be a dangerous route to take, even though everything within us often screams the opposite. One of my favorite lines from the Navy SEALS is "Moderation is for cowards." This excites us, and inwardly we jump up, exclaiming our agreement. But "all things in moderation" is really the better and more sustainable life practice.

Being overcommitted to the pursuit is an equally dangerous pitfall. In contrast to the pitfall of elevation, the recipient of this danger is *yourself*. When there is no room or time made for necessary recovery, you will slowly but surely break down. Regardless of how important commitment is, there still needs to be a *balance*. Stress and recovery go hand in hand, similar to yin and yang.

4. *The Pitfall of Emotions*

The last pitfall worth mentioning is another form of imbalance: running purely off of emotions. Emotions are a great thing, but they aren't always trustworthy or accurate. Because of this, they should *not* be the source of our decision-making. Anytime we commit to a direction or path based largely, if not entirely, on a personal feeling, be prepared for a bumpy ride.

One thing is for certain: When emotions are your captain, you will experience definite mountain-top highs and unbearably deep lows. This chaotic climbing and drastic falling will, over time, zap the life out of you. We aren't meant to be in a constant state of flux. Our bodies are designed to always be moving towards, and maintaining, a state of homeostasis.

As the legendary philosopher Plato once said, "If the chariot is the body, the horses are our emotions, and the rider is our mind—if the horses are dragging the rider against his will, danger is coming." Just like horses, emotions aren't a bad thing; they're actually a great thing. But they are wild, and oftentimes they have a mind of their own. As riders, we mustn't punish or abuse the horses but rather use them to help us get where we want to go. Emotions must be directed toward where we are going and corrected when they start leading us astray.

The point is not to ignore, avoid, or punish your emotions but rather to use your emotions for benefit rather than detriment. Use them to fuel what you do, but let your rational and logical mind inform you of the correct path to travel.

THE FRUIT OF THE LABOR

> *"If it scares you, it might be a good thing to try."*
> —Seth Godin

Setting life trajectories can be intimidating. Daunting tasks make us want to shrink back into our shell of comfort so that we don't have to weather the unavoidable storms ahead. But where's the fun in that? And more important, where's the life in that?

Undoubtedly, there are a vast number of people who will be content with mediocrity. They will be okay with pursuing security and comfort above all else. Their level of commitment will typically match their level of ambition, with both average at best. The fact that you're reading this book helps you understand that this does not describe who *you* are. In his beautiful and heart-wrenching auto-biography, Paul Kalanithi posed the question, "If the unexamined life was not worth living, was the unlived life worth examining?" To truly *live*, life takes commitment.

No matter the endeavor, we won't be our best if we aren't 100 percent committed. There are undoubtedly times when commitment is easier to obtain than others, but true commitment lasts in both the calm and the storm.

The last comment to make is that being committed does involve using your brain. There are real obstacles we'll face. Some will be external—outside of our control—whereas others will be internally generated of no fault other than our own. Every self-generated roadblock stems from the root of fear or doubt, and these often produce false assumptions about commitment itself, painting it in a negative light. There are many ways we can pervert the purity of commitment, falling prey to both the inherent dangers and the self-inflicted pitfalls.

Moving isn't always safe. Settling for stagnation brings the benefit of security and eliminates the presence of risk. Yet, the nature of life makes risk unavoidable. When we ceaselessly work to eliminate all risk, we are simultaneously eliminating our life (figuratively speaking). Commitment is risky.

But it's worth it.

Seth had a few more poignant words for this path to mastery; he said, "There are only three choices—you're either moving forward, falling behind, or standing still. To succeed, to get to that light at the end of the tunnel, you've got to make some sort of forward progress, no matter how small" (*The Dip*, p. 69). We must take a step, moving in the direction we are committed to, living the life we are called to.

Commitment is an honorable pursuit. And the fruit of this labor? *Belief.* Belief is the secret sauce that emboldens and empowers you with the strength to move mountains. And who doesn't want to do that?

LEARNING

"Education is knowing what to do when you don't know."

−A STUDENT OF DANIEL KAHNEMAN

"Tell me and I forget, teach me and I may remember, involve me and I learn."

−BENJAMIN FRANKLIN

MY STORY

WHEN I BECAME A LEARNER

From an early age, I was considered a smart kid. I was particularly quick in picking up new concepts and, being competitive, I had a knack for always trying to be the best. Was this something I was born with? Probably. Did this give me a leg up in the early days? For sure. And when you start ahead, the gap only widens over time.

But there's a shocking element to this story: I didn't learn how to "learn" until half-way through college—honestly.

Early on in life, learning came naturally. Curiosity was the driving force behind picking up new ideas; and as a child, curiosity runs deep in your veins. Every situation offers an adventure with something new to discover. Life is rich with the world forever at your fingertips. My favorite experiences throughout childhood always involved some sort of mischief-making with friends, usually starting with a what-if proposition.

This natural form of learning propels us to accumulate information and knowledge at a rapid rate. When I learned I was a fairly smart kid, I realized that school would naturally be easier for me than for most others. I assumed this was a luxury that would leave me with more time for fun things—like playing golf. As I got better and better at school, I got worse and worse at learning. The end sum of becoming good at school is getting good grades with less effort. Efficiency replaced usefulness, and all the while I was blissfully ignorant of the seeds I was sowing.

Fast forward to my time at college and not much had changed, except for the arena of golf. After growing up in Kansas, the move to California provided an entirely new field of golfers to compete against. Along with added competition, there were now new courses (and course styles), new environments, and new challenges. I was swimming in a much bigger pond than high school, and was receiving much more input and instruction than ever before. As I fought to become comfortable in a brand-new environment, I saw for the first time, how little I knew and how much I needed to learn if I was going to have success on the golf course.

With the wealth of knowledge my collegiate coach had to offer, I committed to becoming as sponge-like as possible, soaking up every ounce of information thrown my way. This opened up a whole new world, uncovering the vast complexities of the game of golf, expanding day by day. The more I learned, the more that I saw I needed to learn. And that's when my eyes were finally opened...

This wasn't just a need reserved for the golf course; this was a need present in the classroom as well. And beyond the classroom, it was an integral part of all of life—especially in careers and endeavors to come. What golf finally highlighted wasn't merely a golf issue; it was a life issue. I needed to learn how to learn.

CONCEPT

THE QUICK FIX

New Year's resolutions and diets are two helpful illustrations of the idea that's related to this concept of learning.

Both diets and New Year's resolutions have been popular for ages, but it's not because of the product or idea itself. Rather, it's because of the promise it makes: this *one* thing will drastically change all other parts of your life. What diet doesn't promise the illusive result of body, mind, and life transformation? And in the realm of New Year's resolutions, the whole idea behind them is, "What *one thing* will drastically change or improve my life if committed to for an entire year?" We desperately want this to be true, which is why we will commit to believing it is true, time and time again, until our inner motivation runs dry and we fall back to square one.

But there is some truth to these claims. If we were able to be disciplined enough to stick to the strict eating plans, that discipline would naturally carry over to other areas of life where discipline may also be lacking. As long as we persisted, this domino effect would continue forward, resulting in the miraculous transformation often depicted in infomercials and website testimonials. It isn't the advertised thing itself, but rather the compounding nature of that one thing.

Keep this in mind when you read my next statement: Learning *is* that one thing—the quick fix. If we learn how to learn, then there's nothing we won't be able to learn. It's simple! It's the ultimate life hack.

At it's core, learning is simple. But just because something is easily understood does *not* mean it's easily accomplished. Simple does *not* mean easy. In fact, the premise of learning is the exact opposite. When it comes to learning that lasts, **the path of most resistance equals the path of most learning**.

STARTED AT THE TOP, NOW WE'RE HERE

How can that be true? Why does learning have to be so hard? If we are naturally good learners as kids, then why can't we be naturally good learners as adults?

The truth is, ever since our youth we have been on a downward slide—the slide of unlearning how to learn.

In the transition from adolescence into adulthood, a change takes place in our brain. We move from a curious and adventurous mindset, seeing every situation as an opportunity to learn something new, to a mindset operating largely off of past memories and skills learned through repetition. Stated another way: as we grow up, our brains categorize and discard situations or information we've already encountered, freeing up our mind to consciously think about more important things in the present moment. This is helpful for getting more accomplished and building upon what we already know, but this comes with a trade-off. In resorting to default processing, we gradually diminish our ability to truly and effectively learn *new* things.

What started as our natural mindset (learning) has steadily become an unnatural one. This transition is beneficial for humanity by allowing us to move past the elementary understandings of childhood and into the mature functioning and intellectualized reasoning of adulthood. Without this shift our world wouldn't be the same. But just because we have graduated from taking baths as a child to taking showers as an adult, that doesn't mean we should throw the baby out with the bath water. As a friend of mine poignantly stated, "We should always strive to be child-like, *not* childish." Adults can take baths too, you know.

The question that remains is, where did we go wrong? How did we so effectively unlearn what we so competently began with? What were the catalysts that stunted our learning abilities and created our developmental stagnation?

It is something far more systemic than you might think.

EDUCATION IS NOT OUR TUTOR

Whenever we hear someone talk about "learning," we immediately associate it, by default, with education (myself included). The inner assumption at play is that *learning* was accomplished through our education, and now our careers are the time in life reserved for the *doing*.

Let's evaluate this assumption by first looking at some definitions.

Education is described as "the process of receiving or giving systematic instruction, especially at a school or university." Another definition is "the act or process of imparting or acquiring general knowledge, developing the powers of reasoning and judgment, and generally of preparing oneself or others intellectually for mature life." All of these goals that education aims to accomplish are helpful and honorable.

But, if we honestly reflect on our own experience within the edu-cational system, how often do we, unassumingly, associate *receiving* an education with the *act* of learning?

Education is a vital part of any thriving society. It provides a foun-dation for equal opportunities regardless of your background. This is never perfectly portrayed or practiced, but that is always the goal of education, by and large. As individuals, we need to be taught general knowledge, we need to understand and develop "the powers of reason-ing and judgment," and we should all strive to be "generally prepared" for an "intellectually mature life." These are worthy and noble pursuits.

The danger lies in thinking that receiving an education automatical-ly means we all know how to learn.

A GIFT OR A FIGHT?

Language is important, and the words chosen to portray that language matter.

Why is it we refer to education as something we *receive*? Receiving something denotes that (1) it is a gift, and (2) it is something we passive-ly acquire/accomplish.

In any system of giving, there are always opportunities to abuse the structure for personal gain. Education is no exception. The goal for edu-cation from the "givers" (providers) is to facilitate a provision of general knowledge to the masses—striving to reach the highest number of stu-dents while doing the best job possible in educating them; striving for both quality and quantity, albeit an impossible feat to simultaneously achieve. The goal for education from the "receivers" (students) is simply to earn good grades.

So while the givers of education have good intentions in providing an educational structure for success and growth, these structures create and promote different motivations for the receivers of that education. The student's mindset is almost entirely given to the task of "receiving good grades." This is an obvious disconnect. As a student, you can be a professional grade-getter while still remaining a complete novice in the department of learning. Much of this disconnect can be attributed to the system that's been created. As writer and author Ta-Nehisi Coates aptly stated, "Schools [are] not concerned with curiosity, they're concerned with compliance."

In contrast to education, learning is an action. It requires *doing*.

Learning is defined as "the acquisition of knowledge or skills through experience, study, or by being taught." The key differential between learning and education is the state in which it takes place—one is passive, and the other is active. Education is merely received—a passive action. Learning is the *active* reception of information, skills, or knowledge. It is an effortful action that, once acquired, solidifies as a part of our being.

Simply put, learning is a *fight*.

NOT WHAT YOU WANT, THINK, OR FEEL

And this leads to the realization that **learning is counterintuitive**, which makes sense in a weird way.

Human beings have an oversized propensity towards laziness. As we grow into maturity, we must grow in our awareness of where this laziness is manifested. When it comes to learning, the habits we form during our education will carry on unless they are replaced. This is detrimental to our capacity for learning because, as we found earlier, education is often viewed as a game of getting good grades. The easiest way to accomplish this is by mass repetition, memory-blitzing, and last-second cramming (not to mention the ethics-removed version called cheating).

Some of these habits may even be encouraged by teachers throughout the education system because of their effectiveness in the short-term. But, as with most things in life, short-term gain will sacrifice long-term reward. The gain is good grades; the reward lost is the ability to effectively learn.

We all want learning to be easy. We all desire for the path of least resistance to be the path that benefits us most. We all want laziness to be rewarding. It just isn't true.

When it comes to learning well, the obstacle *is* the way forward. The more effort—specifically mental effort—the more we learn, and the better we learn.

ESSENTIAL INGREDIENT

In addition to learning being strenuous, an active pursuit, counterintuitive, and a fight, there's one final description to highlight in regard to learning. And to make this point, I want to look to the arena of cooking.

Cooking is an art. It takes individual components that, by themselves, are not very appetizing or satisfying, and combines them together to create a final product that brings our palette pleasure beyond imagination.

Like any art form, cooking takes practice. You must gain an understanding of what tastes good with what, both intellectually (by learning common cooking knowledge/practices) and experientially (by tasting the effects). After gaining some cooking experience, you soon come to discover several key ingredients. These ingredients are the components that make or break a food dish. While they may be small in stature, their effect is massive. Without their inclusion, the other ingredients simply can't make up for their absence. For example:

- Sugar for chocolate-chip cookies
- Pumpkin for pumpkin pie
- Cinnamon for cinnamon rolls
- Powdered sugar for frosting
- Cream for ice cream
- Tomatoes for marinara sauce
- Corn starch for gravy
- Chili powder for chili

These can be called *essential ingredients*.

The point of this illustration is to say that **learning is that essential ingredient** required for the creation and cultivation of skill, talent, or proficiency throughout all of life. Ultimately, it is a required element in the path of mastery. Without it, we will forever be stuck in a cycle of repeated behaviors and regurgitated knowledge/skill. With it, all aspects of our lives are magnified and expanded.

To go one step further, learning is the essential ingredient with the greatest compounding effect. To test this point, look at the reverse: what are the compounding effects of *not* having strong learning abilities? If you are not able to *truly* learn, then you will end up becoming very skilled at repeating tasks or processes. As a result, you will have a very narrow range of proficiency that is specific to your current job or field of work. Thus, there is virtually zero capacity for transference of skills into other arenas of life. If the point in time comes when you feel called to a different job or type of work, then you will have no other option than to begin at the bottom rung of the food-chain ladder. This is often incentive enough to keep people in jobs that are utterly dissatisfying and unfulfilling. And beyond career-specific ramifications, life will be filled with greater fear of change (since change means you have to *learn* a new way of life), fear of failure, and a stubborn obstinance toward any worldview, experience, or way of thinking outside your own.

Learning is the essential ingredient, the key that opens the door to our pursuit of mastery. Mastery itself can only be accomplished through an abundance of learning; there's simply no other way. It isn't something that is handed to you. It isn't something that will come easily or always be natural for you. But it will always serve you best to have learning as a personal strength, because the benefits of learning will accrue either way—either helping you on your path to mastery or furthering the divide between where you are and where you want to go. The choice is up to you.

Being able to learn well has far-reaching effects beyond the singular subject or skill you are trying to learn. The compounding effects stretch into all aspects of relationships, careers, and life itself. It's a skill that deserves our lifelong devotion. And you better believe it's worth the fight.

Now it's time to learn *how* to fight.

APPLICATION

It is important to lay the foundation for (1) why learning is an innate ability in everyone, (2) why learning is often *un*learned throughout our education, and (3) why we now have to *fight* to regain our learning muscles. Without an understanding of the context surrounding learning, we won't accurately know how we got to this point, and furthermore, we won't know how to get to where we want to go. In seeing our current condition, we now have to *learn* how to help ourselves.

LEARNING AS YOUR IDENTITY

Throughout our lives, we tend to acquire various titles that help define who we are. These usually take root in our younger years, and, if they persist long enough (and if we personally believe them to be true), then they may last a lifetime. Maybe you were good at arts and crafts as a child, so you decided to pursue more fine arts through your high school years, acquiring the title of a "creative." If you end up pursuing a career path in some creative field, then this title will last your whole life. And even if you didn't pursue a creative career but took a different path, then you may have chosen to keep the title of a creative within whatever you do. The same is true for athletes. Once an athlete, always an athlete, despite that title carrying an obvious and universal decline throughout your life.

Titles are a form of self-identification. We identify ourselves with the people who we view ourselves to be. Identities can be either agreeable or contentious based on the truthfulness of the claims they make. But with certain aspects of our identity, we have a say in how we want to be known.

An identity that should be esteemed and desired by every reader of this book is that of a "learner." Some argue that we are at our peak as "learners" during our childhood, learning about all the exciting things life has to offer. While this is true, learning is an identity we can maintain (and improve!) throughout our *entire* lives. The goal is not to momentarily acquire the title of "proficient learner" as a child, or in various seasons of life such as college or the beginning of a career. We must aim to earn the honorable title of being known as a "lifelong learner."

HOW TO EARN THE TITLE OF "LEARNER"

Identities are made and titles are earned based on the goals we set and the actions we take. If we desire to become lifelong learners, then we must develop the habits and practices to make those goals become the reality of our life. Here are some big-picture suggestions to help achieve this reality:

Try New Things

In order to be a lifelong learner, you must continue to learn throughout your life. The logic is simple. Learning requires interacting with either (1) new components within your current job, career, or skill set, or (2) completely new encounters. More often than not, option 2 is much easier to consistently accomplish in the endless world of possibilities.

So make it a priority to try something new every month. It sounds daunting at first, but once we see the benefit we receive in return, it becomes a joy instead of a burden. Anytime we establish a new habit, we have to expend more effort to follow through with the desired discipline than we would like. But the more habits and skills we acquire, the better we get at acquiring them. The more we learn, the better we get at learning. And the more we learn, the more comfortable we are with new things and the more we enjoy the process of learning itself.

This is yet another example of learning's compounding nature. Get the ball moving and then allow momentum to propel you even further.

Bottom line: get good at trying new things.

Become a Bucket List Doer

Sure, anyone can create a bucket list, and most people do. But how many people actually cross off their hopes, dreams, and wishes as an experienced reality? The percentage is not high.

Spending time daydreaming about what we *actually* want to do with our lives is a fun activity, but then comes the part of actually doing them. This can bring much trepidation, even from the simple thought of trying it.

Usually, life is to blame. So many things get in the way of us accomplishing our wildest hopes and dreams. "That's just the reality of life," we say. But are you being honest with yourself? Do you truly want to make it happen? Or would you rather just sit and dream about it? Bucket lists are not for the bookshelf to collect dust until you finally retire in old age. Bucket lists are for your youth, mid-life, and old age alike. Some (like heli-skiing) may be better accomplished in the younger years, whereas others (like writing a book) may be more suited for the later years.

Bucket lists are helpful when thinking about how we can incorporate learning into our lives. Oftentimes we write down new activities we've never done but have always wanted to do (like bungee jumping for me). In essence, this is learning: doing an activity we have never done before and learning it through experience.

You've heard it before, but the first step forward is always the hardest. So make it easy and help yourself out. Pick a skill or trait that you desperately want, and more importantly, one that's connected to your larger purpose and path in life, and then go do it. Make it happen. You won't regret it. In fact, you can use that as ammo—reminding yourself that you're never disappointed in doing what you truly want to do.

All the while, you'll be laying down the tracks for a lifelong pursuit of learning.

Look to the Experts
Learning something new is a strenuous and difficult task. So it makes sense to do all we can to make the path easier. In modern society, there will always be an expert—someone who has been through the journey of mastery and has unlocked the keys to the kingdom. They've put in the manual labor, laying down the foundational bricks so that the road is sturdier and more accessible for all who want to follow.

When learning, seek out experts within the field or space you are entering, thus shortening the time you'll need to gain your footing. These experts will provide invaluable information regarding best practices, experiences, and the pitfalls to avoid when learning. They've both walked the walk and talked the talk.

So start listening and start following.

Be a Reader and a Doer
This ties back to the concept of the two forms of learning already mentioned: informational and experiential. When we read books, we are inputting new information that facilitate some level of learning (or entertainment). When we pick up a golf club for the first time on the driving range, we are inputting new information into our brains by the movement and experience of our body trying to hit a little white ball.

Many times, the intellectual and experiential worlds intersect, and at these points we can learn to a greater degree by understanding both the head knowledge and the body knowledge. These spheres don't have to be segregated, and we benefit from seeking to marry the two practices for each learning goal we have.

One is not inherently better than the other. Both are needed.

Love the Challenge

A challenge requires doing something that tests our ability, a demanding endeavor. Within life, we are constantly creating habits. Some are good but many are bad, especially if we aren't consciously directing them.

Focused persistence on developing a habit of doing hard things will allow us to live a life of learning. The place we should be most afraid of is the comfort zone. The longer we remain in our comfort zone, the more opposed we are to leaving that zone, and the scarier it will be when we finally take the leap of faith *out* of our comfort zone.

Help yourself out: embrace the challenge. Love the discomfort. Jump out of your box.

Inquire More

Asking questions is a developed skill, which is funny seeing that children ask the most questions of all—and often the most profoundly clarifying ones at that.

So why are we so bad at asking questions? Maybe we think we've got it all figured out already. But if we have it all figured out, then how can we learn? We can't. Or, more importantly - *we won't*.

We all have something to share. Your life has given you both intellectual and experiential knowledge that differs from your sibling, or the cashier at the grocery store, or your physical therapist, or your regional manager, or your next-door neighbor. If you want to develop into a lifelong learner, then learn to ask better questions. Every day we have countless interactions with people who have something to share. Whether or not it is ever shared is up to you.

Seek to redeem the time spent interacting with these humans by developing a habit of asking *intentional* and *purposeful* questions. It is surprising how much you learn simply by asking a thoughtful question of one person a day. Chances are, they will have specific knowledge or experience in an area that you don't. What a great opportunity to *learn*.

So get to asking.

Patience
Learning takes time; it simply doesn't happen overnight. The same is true with forming and developing habits. Yet the more we develop the good habit of learning, the better we get at doing so.

We always need the reminder to be patient, because the second you put this book down, the inspiration that may have sprung up will get confronted with the realities of daily life: the to-do lists, job duties, personal responsibilities, relational obligations, and on and on it goes. Patience is needed because our emotions fluctuate, and the way we feel won't always be compatible with learning something new. Patience is needed because baby steps take a long time to finally get somewhere.

It's a long life we live (if we're blessed with a typical life span), so put your nose to the learning grindstone, and strive to always maintain a patient perspective.

Play the long game.

Momentum Is Your Friend
Learning is best done intelligently. The smarter we learn, the faster we become smart. This takes self-awareness. No one knows yourself better than you do.

It is important to recognize what time of day you learn best, or what atmosphere facilitates your best focus, or what method fits your personality. Once you know how to best operate, you can then cater to those situations and capitalize on your learning aptitude by planting seeds in the most fertile soil.

Momentum is a very real thing in life (more on that to come), so start using the slope to gain more speed, propelling you toward your end goal. In the same way as knowing when you learn best, so too you will need to know when you *don't* learn best. This means recognizing when recovery is needed versus adding more stress or input.

Guess what? That's something you have to *learn* too. Funny how it all connects.

HELPING OURSELVES

Now that we've worked through the big-picture strategies and approaches to learning well, it's time to take a closer look at the individual tools and tricks to help us learn as efficiently and effectively as possible.

With entire books written on becoming better learners, this section will merely be a condensed list of the overall strategies that assist in the process. (For a deeper dive into this art form [learning], read *Make It Stick* by Peter Brown.)

- Repetition—
  - o While this plays a part, it's not the same as the mass repetition commonly prescribed through the education system. Rather, it is a *mentally engaged* repetition.
- Recollection—
  - o Recalling information from the annals of our mind is an action that takes *effort*. If you don't sweat when you go to the gym, then you probably aren't accomplishing anything. The same is true with your mind.
- Patience—
  - o Allowing space for time to pass between attempts at recollection will create a stronger connection between the idea/information and our brain. This is another example of the relationship between benefit and effort.
- Connections—
  - o Taking new information and relating it to concepts and ideas already learned will facilitate better memory of the new additions. (Think of meeting someone for the first time. If you have a mutual friend, then the chances that you will remember their name or who they are will increase by a considerable amount.)

- Reduction—
  - o Reducing the amount of information you intake will help facilitate more effective acquisition. Less is more—quality over quantity.
- Regurgitate—
  - o Utilize outlets to assist you in the process of recollection and synthesizing. This could include conversations with others or personal times of clarification through journaling and writing.
- Deconstruction—
  - o This is breaking the big-picture skill, idea, or concept into smaller and more easily digestible pieces. Knowing how the individual parts work will always result in a greater knowledge of the whole.
- Incentivize—
  - o Have clear and concise goals. Make it challenging enough for yourself but not too challenging that it becomes insurmountable or seemingly unachievable. Find the sweet spot and then use your weaknesses to your advantage by attaching negative incentives to provide extra motivation for accomplishing the task.
- Intention—
  - o Ensure that the skill, idea, or concept is attached to your greater purpose (your why). This increases both the joy and steadfastness in the midst of the *fight* of learning. Knowing the intention behind what we are learning makes the battles we face worth it.
- Trust—
  - o In all things, we must *fully* trust the process. Learning is a process that takes both time and effort. It doesn't happen overnight, and it doesn't happen without some blood, sweat, and tears. It requires a lot of patience with a maintained focus on the long-term reward from the short-term sacrifice of effortful learning.

- Maintenance—
  - o For skills to be accessible long-term, we must dedicate re-trieval time throughout the years ahead. This is the needed maintenance for the ground gained in order to facilitate life-long aptitude.

These strategies are useful on their own, but the real power lies in the ability to comprehensively incorporate them all, with an emphasis on the specific components that are most needed in light of your personal weaknesses.

HURTING OURSELVES

As with any part of life, there are ways we can help ourselves and many other ways we end up hurting ourselves, both knowingly and unknow-ingly. Many times we end up pursuing the wrong path without knowing it. Other times, we're just lazy and don't want to do the work needed. And then there are extremists who always swing the pendulum too far to the other side of a healthy balance. What helps most in avoiding self-inflicted harm is awareness. The goal of this section is to help us see the ways we go astray so that we can better recognize them and then readjust, returning to the path of true learning.

So, here are the ways we often hinder our ability to learn:

Perfectionism
This harmful approach refuses to accept any outcome short of perfec-tion. It is a prevalent malady, often viewed as a desirable trait. The logic is that if the product that results isn't a perfect representation of the goal we had, then we have to keep working at it until we get there. The fallacy comes in thinking that we will ever fully arrive. News flash! We won't.

At it's core, perfectionism is a self-limiting belief that stems from fear—the fear of failing, the fear of not reaching the Mt. Everest heights we imag-ined for ourselves. It's seeing our inability to reach the peak of all our hopes and dreams as a total failure rather than the accomplishment of how much ground we were able to cover and the progress we made along the way.

The worst aspect of this misplaced belief is its reciprocal nature. When we, who are by nature imperfect, aspire to the level of perfec-tion, then we set ourselves up for failure by creating an unattainable goal. When we don't live up to our own impractical standards of excellence, we simultaneously assume the title of a failure while doubling down on our efforts of attaining the unattainable the next time around. Pretty soon, this cycle of failing and then doubling down will lead to a deep-seated fear of failure, crippling and preventing us from ever pursuing a worthwhile goal or endeavor beyond our current capacities.

The recipe for stagnation is found in never reaching beyond your current capabilities. In the kitchen of perfectionism, you will quickly become a one-trick pony, and nobody wants mac 'n' cheese for the rest of their lives.

Comparison
In one sense, comparison can be a helpful habit. On a fundamental level, we are all human beings, which means we all start from a theoretically level playing field. But of course, that is purely in theory. In reality, we are shaped and formed by the context and background of our individual lives. And that is where comparison can cause harm—in not understanding the need for comparison to be tapered by context.

A good illustration for this is professional athletes. When we see an athlete as dominant as Usain Bolt, or Tiger Woods, or Michael Jordan, we naturally view them as supreme *individual* talents. We assume they have superior natural talent and skills, paired with the steadfast and obsessive work ethic needed to reach the status of greatness. There is definite truth in this assumption, but the reality often ignored or unseen is the cohort of individuals, coaches, trainers, teachers, therapists, managers, and facilitators all combining their expertise to refine the athlete's talent. The fruit of their collective labor are the supernatural feats and record-book accomplishments that all get assigned to one name: the blessed, individual recipient of a glory deserved to be shared by the whole team.

Why else would the quarterback or running back, after scoring a touchdown, instinctively celebrate with his teammates who are on the offensive line? Because, even if no one else in the stadium understands or recognizes their worth, the running back or quarterback know that what they do rests completely on the line's ability to block the enemy's attack.

Back to comparison.

When we look at another's accomplishments, we instinctively compare. The less context we have for another's accomplishments, the less weight we should carry with comparison. Unrealistic comparisons that are created off little to no context create a lower sense of self-worth and cause more harm than good. It skews both our reality and the reality of our comparison.

To sum it up, anytime comparison results in a defeatist mindset of self-doubt and self-loathing, *stop it*. Life's too short to waste time comparing. Start owning who you are and begin learning how to maximize the unique version of you.

Mimicking

This concept is similar to comparison. Mimicking means copying what another individual does in order to reach the same level of competency or accomplishment. Again, this is not entirely bad, but it can produce less-than-desirable results.

Mimicking specific individuals is always riskier than following the widely accepted principles of larger populations (industry standards). I know what you're thinking: *More risk equals more reward*. And you're right! But when we start copying the technique and routines of specific individuals, we take on the risk of not being an ideal fit for that certain style or mannerism. This is where awareness of your internal wirings and the context behind your targeted individual become determinants of the success (or failure) that follows.

Mimicking, specifically in relation to learning, can also be detrimental. This will be discussed at length in chapters 4 and 7, but the premise is that everyone learns differently and at different rates. Just because another person can learn a skill in two months doesn't mean it won't take you twelve months to do the same.

Overvaluation

This is connected to the concept of balance. Learning is a great tool. It's a desirable and honorable goal to pursue, and it can have an amazing effect on the rest of your life and the work you produce. But that all rests on the premise that you're actually producing work.

When learning is not proportionately valued, its usefulness begins to decline. For learning to be useful, it must have an end goal—something that will result once it's been accomplished. This has to do with the intersection of experience and knowledge.

Seeking knowledge is important for understanding the purpose behind what we do. Being an informed and intentional individual, who acts with conviction and purpose based on beliefs and ideas that are well thought out and logically formed, is important. But knowledge has its limits, and if everyone in the world pursued only the acquisition of knowledge, then nothing would ever be accomplished—namely, the vital skills and systems for human life and preservation (hunting, gathering, building shelter, sanitation and hygiene, etc.). Paul Kalanithi said it best: "If the unexamined life was not worth living, was the unlived life worth examining?"

Learning doesn't take place solely in the mind. It takes place in actions, in movements, in physical efforts, and in life experiences. If you solely learn from experience, then you will lack the ability to critically think through the meaning and purpose of your life beyond the current situation and circumstances. If you solely learn from knowledge, then you will be in a perpetual state of discourse over the meaning behind everyday actions, so much so that you never get to the point of action itself.

Experience errs on the side of others, whereas knowledge errs on the side of self. Both are needed, but a balance must be struck. The danger comes when the value placed on learning itself exceeds our foundation: the purpose for why we are learning in the first place.

Never lose your anchor.

Overexcitement

Anytime we embark on learning a new skill, concept, or idea, we become giddy with excitement. It's similar to Christmas Eve as a first grader—the beauty of the colorfully wrapped packages keeping us awake till the first crack of sunlight Christmas morn. *Giddy!*

In golf, it's the "new club" syndrome. If you've been struggling with your putter, the natural assumption is that it's the club's fault (not the user of that club). So you decide to take a look at the new shiny putters in the pro shop. One catches your eye and you decide to give it a try. What's the harm in giving it a test ride anyway? The next 30 minutes you magically transform into the Ben Crenshaw of old (one of the best put-ters in history). You literally can't miss a putt if you tried. That evening you drive home with a new addition to your golf bag—and a smaller bank account to match.

This is a cyclical process, repeating itself time and time again. The excitement of something new and shiny makes us lose our grasp of reali-ty. We feel as if the cure to all our putting-cancers has finally been found, and with the new addition our golf game will be unstoppable. Chances are, in less than a few weeks time you will find yourself back to your consistently inconsistent self with the putter in hand.

Learning any new skill or idea gives us the same misconception. It begins with oversized expectations paired with misplaced self-con-fidence. We begin planning all of the future possibilities of being an expert in such field and place an unhealthy amount of confidence in our underdeveloped and untested position as a novice.

Usually, the fallout comes from taking too big a piece of the pie. We take on more information than our brains can hold. We try to be an ex-pert in every aspect of the job instead of focusing on one at a time. The pie looks and smells so good that we trick ourselves into thinking our body wants to consume it all. Stomachaches ensue.

Patience is required in any journey of learning. Sustainability is the unsexy but proven method of growth needed for success. "Baby steps to greatness" is the motto. In the beginning, each day should be about taking one step forward, not running a mile. Eventually, the aspiration of running a mile, or even multiple miles in a day, is a good thing. But at the beginning it can be deadly.

Gluttony
This is a similar concept to overexcitement, but it differs in when it ap-pears during the process of learning. Typically we are overexcited at the beginning of learning something new. Yet, as with food, we can be gluttonous as adults just as easily as children. The difference is, adults should know better.

Gluttony is best seen in the concept of all-you-can-eat buffets. Typ-ically, we pay a certain amount higher than normal to participate in the feast that is known as buffets. Due to the extra money spent, we feel obligated to eat above and beyond what our stomach (and heart) desires. By the end of the feast, we leave wishing we could voluntarily vomit in order to provide our bodies with space and relief.

The assumption in these situations is that the amount of food you eat determines the amount of discount you receive with the price you paid for the buffet. The problem is, what you paid never changes.

When learning, we often fall prey to this same false reality. It is such a natural thought process to assume: the amount of information I consume equals the amount of information I learn. Yet nothing could be further from the truth. Information has a tendency to produce diminishing returns. As we noted earlier, effective learning is not the same as cramming into our minds as much information as possible. As with food and the body, when our brains becomes overloaded with more information than we can properly digest, it will discard the excess without gaining benefit from the oversized input.

Excess is the exception and not the rule. In reality, we can process and absorb much less information than we think. Just as ingraining movements and muscle memory into our myelin (sheath-lining nerve fibers involved with carrying out movements) takes countless repetitions, so too does accurately and effectively learning new information and ideas.

Simply put, when it comes to learning, less is more.

THE END OF THE MATTER

At the end of the day, learning is all about motives.

If your motive in learning is to make yourself look good, or to learn for learning's sake, or associating meaning in life with the pursuit of knowledge, then chances are, you will experience the calamities learning can bring.

If your motive in learning is to develop yourself for the purpose of serving others and benefiting the world we live in, or to gain proficiency within a field to do the best job you possibly can, or because you understand learning's rightful place as a component of living a successful life, not *the* component, then chances are, it will be a self-fulfilling prophecy.

Again, this is a part of the process that must be viewed as that—a piece of the greater puzzle that is your life. It must be seen as a part of the whole, important but not absolute. We achieve this by putting learning under the umbrella of our overarching purpose in life—our why. If you are able to do that, then learning will do nothing other than benefit your progress in life.

Phase Two: Complexity

4

TEACHABILITY (& DISCERNMENT)

"It is not until we have truly been shocked into seeing ourselves as we really are, instead of as we wish or hopefully assume we are, that we can take the first step toward individual reality."

—EDWARD WHITMOUNT

"Don't believe everything that you think."

—BJ MILLER

"The sign of intelligence is that you are constantly wondering. Idiots are always dead sure about every thing they are doing in their life."

—VASUDEV

MY STORY

FALLING INTO TEACHABILITY

I'm not sure why, but teachability came easy for me—most likely because *it works.*

When I graduated high school, I headed out to the West Coast for college at The Master's University, just north of Los Angeles, CA. Being from small-town U.S.A. (Hutchinson, Kansas), this was a big move. I knew I was stepping into a much bigger pond than I'd ever known, which naturally brings the shrinking of my own relative size. If I was to thrive (let alone survive) in my new environment, then I would need all the help I could get.

This mindset was fertile soil, a soil ripe for the seeds of teachableness. This understanding allowed me to have humility to see that I needed the help of others to get where I wanted to go. It helped me see that I really didn't know it all. Unbeknownst to me, the migration to a bigger pond paid off in much bigger ways than I ever could have imagined at 18 years old.

I say "unbeknownst" because truly that was the reality. During the four years of playing under Coach Jason, there were several times where he made the comment that I was "one of the most coachable players he had ever taught." This surprised me. I hadn't realized I possessed this desirable trait that so sneakily seeped into my being. I never consciously planned on being teachable; it was more of a necessity for survival.

Slowly but surely, I grew in my awareness of this trait, beginning to see its beauty and blessing. The people who surrounded me during those four years at college had so much to teach and share, and there was so much I needed to learn and not nearly enough time to learn it all. Only by learning from the experience of others would I be able to leapfrog some of the years needed to arrive at the destination I desired. This applied not only to the game of golf and the infinite intricacies within the sport but also to life and what it means to grow into a responsible, ambitious, confident, humble, God-fearing human being.

In reflecting on my time in college, I can confidently say that the greatest and longest-lasting impact of those four years was the guidance given from mentors, coaches, and other influential people/peers in my life. And that was something I just fell into.

DISCOVERING DISCERNMENT

As I transitioned into my professional career, I finally became cognizant of the benefit of teachability and made it my aim to take full advantage of it in my growth as a player. The problem is, as skill set and understanding grow, the layers and layers of complexities grow in a parallel fashion. (Remind you of anything?)

This natural progression on the road to mastery caused me to start chasing the wind, a frivolous endeavor that's more confusing than clarifying. Suddenly there were countless voices to listen too, endless examples of "success" to look to and learn from, coming in every shape, size, and color imaginable. Every perceived breakthrough seemed to lead to a dead end, and I was left grasping after the illusive nature of a successful performance.

This was confusing.

Wasn't I supposed to be teachable? Wasn't this the key to growth? Why are there so many conflicting voices and ideas? Isn't there *one* correct path? Who was it who lost the magical blueprint to success?

Alongside this confusion, I had established a platform for vulnerability. This platform was my website.

In creating a website for my professional golf career and brand, my goal was to keep family, friends, and fans up to date with the happenings and results of my golf career. It was an important part of my journey, and one that produced many unintended benefits for my personal development. But, along with the good that it brought came some bad. In providing raw and honest information on how I was performing and what went on in my headspace, I simultaneously opened the door for any and all feedback that those following had to offer.

This open invitation to comments and advice created even more inner turmoil, as I continued on in my search for how to crack the code and rewrite the lost blueprint for success as a professional golfer. It didn't make sense.

And that was when discernment came knocking on my door.

Slowly but surely, I began to see the need for discernment and discretion in determining which voices should be heeded and which should be discarded. Just because someone has something to say doesn't mean it's advice that *should* be accepted and integrated. In a similar fashion, just because one professional golfer practiced or played a certain way did not mean that it was the best method for my game. This was my first effort toward cracking open the door to mastery, toward finding the simplicity on the far side of complexity that had remained invisible for so long.

CONCEPT

The last chapter was all about the concept of learning. Learning is a process that's largely (if not entirely) inward-focused. It takes an understanding of our own tendencies, strengths, and weaknesses in order to know the best strategies for successfully acquiring new skills and ideas. Ultimately, we are the ones who have to take the initiative and ownership in cultivating and growing the life skill of learning.

But, as with every aspect of life, a healthy balance needs to be found. Learning shouldn't be only a self-focused endeavor; there needs to be an outward focus as well.

This outward-facing form of learning is called **teachability**.

OTHERS-FOCUSED LEARNING

I want to first make it clear that if we can't (1) understand the process needed and (2) commit to the effort required for effective learning, then we will resort to forever living a spoon-fed life—the life of a infant. This is why *individual* learning is such an important foundation to lay. The onus of learning is always on you.

While learning is the foundation that must be built first, the equally important foundation that follows is teachability—seeing and believing in the value found in *others-focused learning*.

"Teachability" is a word that denotes the ability to be taught, but it also means being *willing* and *able* to learn. It is often used to describe the spirit in which you approach instruction or feedback from others. The object of teachability is your self, but the subject is the person who's instructing you; and what they are providing entails a level of objectivity beyond what you're able to achieve on your own. As Susan Scott said in her book *Fierce Conversations*, "It's not our thoughts or feelings that get us into trouble. It's not our disclosures that cause distress. It's our attachment to them, our belief that we are right." Teachability helps bring an objectivity to our thoughts that allows us to be less attached to them, helping us see them with clearer eyes.

Paired with this objectivity is the reality that the subject (the person teaching you) has a greater understanding or grasp of the skill or knowledge than you do. This duality is the one-two combo a teachable nature provides. Without this spirit of teachability, you can kiss this jab-cross combo goodbye—let alone the kingpin of them all: the jab-cross uppercut.

THE NONNEGOTIABLE

In order to be teachable, there is one nonnegotiable that must be present for you to unlock your ability to be effectively taught.

To keep the boxing theme alive: if objectivity is the cross, and greater competency is the uppercut, then humility is *the jab*.

As a boxer, without an efficient and effective jab, the rest of your combo will be useless. Humility is the jab—the *one* prerequisite that determines your ability (or inability) to learn from others. *Humility*—nothing can replace it, and nothing can compensate in its absence. It is the nonnegotiable element on which the entire "contract" of teachability hinges.

Humility can be defined in many ways. One simple definition is "a modest or low view of one's own importance." It's a word that can be easily communicated or understood but is surprisingly hard to possess. To gain a better grasp of humility, the most practical suggestion I can give you is to pick up the game of golf—seriously.

Golf is a game of inches, excruciatingly so. After gaining enough muscle memory, the focal point of the sport moves from your body to your mind—being played entirely between your two ears. To be a good golfer you *must* possess a high level of confidence. Without confidence, golf cannot be played well. Yet, your confidence will constantly be put to the test. You can hit the perfect tee shot, a beautiful approach shot, and a seemingly perfect putt, but if the putt breaks a fraction more than you thought, then it will catch the lip of the hole and horseshoe right back at you. It's a game of inches.

With the complexities and nuances of golf, it takes a massive amount of experience to become a consistent scorer. But even then there will be bad days. There will be times when you seem to do nothing right. There will be rounds that make you consider giving up the game entirely. It is a sport that forces you into submission, making you admit that you aren't a robot and won't play your best every time you tee it up. If you want practical training on humility, then golf is your greatest tutor.

Beyond golf, I can think of no greater illustration or example of humility than the man Jesus Christ.

If you have not read the Bible before (I would first recommend that you do! At least once), Jesus Christ was God who came to the earth as a man. Imagine this for a moment: picture yourself as God. You just finished creating all the universe, stars, sun and moon, the earth, oceans, animals, and finally you created a man—fashioned in your own likeness. As creator, you brought it all into being and now it is under your dominion. And then there was the fall, when Adam and Eve ate the apple in the Garden of Eden. "Man," your most prized possession, rebelled against you and is now your enemy. What would you do?

I know I would want to wipe out my creation and start over! That is the opposite of what God did. Instead of utterly destroying us, He chose to redeem us—to save us from ourselves. And the way He did this, was by sending His only Son, Jesus Christ, to the earth to live as a man, and to ultimately be killed by man for the sins of man. Humility knows no greater example than this. (See Philippians 2.)

THE ENEMY

Cultivating humility has its fair share of obstacles, but there's one enemy that poses the greatest threat.

Being teachable rests on the premise that you *don't* already know it all. Anyone reading that statement will readily admit they are not the all-encompassing expert within the endless facets of existence and human life. Yet, it becomes much more difficult to readily admit that in everyday situations and interactions.

Why is that? What internal switch is flipped that leads to a closed heart and mind when others try to help us learn or improve?

Enter in public enemy number one: **pride**.

Pride is a self-gratifying monster. It lies within each of us, eagerly awaiting any situation where it can rear its ugly head. When we fall into the habit of feeding it, the monster grows and grows until it is a beast that can't be contained. We become enslaved to the bondage of our own "greatness." We turn our self into the god whom we serve, and all others must bend the knee in subservience.

That is the true downfall of pride. Pride is the belief that we have become God and thus we should be served and praised by all. On the positive side, pride is defined as "a feeling of deep pleasure or satisfaction derived from one's own achievements, the achievements of those with whom one is closely associated, or from qualities or possessions that are widely admired." But rarely is pride a positive influence.

There are many verses throughout the Bible on the perils of pride, but none states it so powerfully and concisely as Proverbs 16:18: "Pride goes before destruction, and a haughty spirit before a fall." This is *wisdom*.

On a practical level, there is no trait that blinds us more than pride. Pride manipulates us to see a false reality. The chief aim of pride is always *self-glorification*. It turns our eyes inward, causing us to lose sight of everything beyond ourself, including the path ahead of us. This is not only perilous but also destructive, especially in our relationships with others.

Teachability rests on understanding that you *can* learn something from the individual who is teaching you. If your starting point is a state of cynical contentiousness (also known as "pride"), then you first have to work to break down the self-created walls of defense in order to see what the other person has to offer.

There really is no greater detriment to our lives than pride. It is seen so clearly by others but is so unwillingly acknowledged by ourself. The more ammunition we have to fight off the damage this inner monster can cause, the better. In this battle, there is no elixir more potent than a spirit of humility—the antonym and direct opposite of pride.

If pride is something you struggle with (and, to differing degrees, it always is), then striving to be teachable can be a great tool and ally to help you help yourself.

HELPING OR HURTING?

Many times we aren't aware of the ways we're hurting ourselves until it's too late.

A good example of this is seen in the weight-room—the gym. After consistently lifting for a period of time, you begin to gain strength and muscle mass. With greater strength, you start adding heavier and heavier weights onto the bar. This is great for self-esteem but not so great for self-preservation. If you've never received training on the proper technique and movement mechanics needed for each specific lift, then the more weight you add, the higher the risk that injuries will result. And injuries don't allow for mulligans.

So here is what **the path of *not* being teachable** looks like.

It begins with the ugly monster of pride (as mentioned earlier), who has an equally cunning and diabolical mistress—ignorance. Where pride is, ignorance surely follows. When these two characteristics are governing your life, it will inevitably produce a narrow perspective. It could even be called a singular perspective—since yours is the only opinion that's allowed credit. This goes hand in hand with a closed-mindedness ripe for blind spots.

"It takes considerable knowledge just to realize the extent of your own ignorance."
—Thomas Sowell

Ultimately, this path elevates self as the priority above all else. We already know that when you become the most important person in the world, a path of destruction is soon to follow, especially with those who are unfortunate enough to be a part of your life. An isolated life is a miserable life. We must fight to keep pride and ignorance from ostracizing us away from our community. Relationships with others is far more important than our relation with ourself.

Conversely, **the path of being teachable** looks a lot brighter.

It starts with the baseline, nonnegotiable of a humble spirit. This means, you actively acknowledge that you *don't* know it all; what results is a natural reduction in personal ignorance, which also guards against our tendency to carry blindspots. This opens the door for gaining true confidence (the helpful sibling of pride) and creates the opportunity for added input—the spirit of teachability.

Ultimately, being teachable enables other people to speak into your life and help you help yourself—by showing you a clearer perspective through an objective lens, one that cannot be acquired on your own.

THE INWARD PROCESS OF TEACHABILITY

Let's expound on what the path of teachability looks like as it plays out in our life.

1. *Core Understanding*—This will be the third time saying this, but it is vital to everything that follows: you must understand (and admit) that there are others who know more than you and that you need their help in order to learn and grow. This is a concept that will continue to be repeated because, unfortunately, it *needs* to be repeated. Fewer and fewer people are striving to be characterized by humility, maintaining an openness and willingness to be taught. Humility is the core foundation for a teachable spirit.

2. *Recognition*—Be aware of the areas in your current knowledge and skillset that are lacking. Then, work on identifying individuals who can provide instruction and assistance in those specific areas. Introspection can help replace unnecessary time spent on trial and error when deciding who will be most useful or effective to learn from.

3. *Association*—Think through the people in your current life or circle to determine who would be most beneficial in a tutor/ mentor relationship, and then approach them with your inquiry. This proposition should not be treated as an afterthought. If you are serious about learning, and understand that time is valuable, then you will demonstrate this by approaching the individual in an intentional and thoughtful way.

4. *Reception*—Once the relationship has begun, you must *receive* the instruction that is given to you. There is no benefit to these relationships if you are constantly arguing and insisting on what *you* believe to be true based on what *you* know. (It's called *others*-centered learning for a reason.) You must seek to understand before you oppose, argue, or disagree—something that applies to all of life, not just teachability.

5. *Incorporation*—Sit with the instruction you've been given. Allow time, experience, interactions, inward thought, reflection, and meditation to help incorporate the instruction into what you do. This will allow it to fully manifest in your life, both personally and purposefully.

6. *Inquisition*—After allowing time for incorporation, it is helpful to return to your tutor/mentor with questions, clarifications, remarks, feedback, and maybe even disagreements. This will help deepen your relationship with them in an honest and genuine way, while facilitating further growth, instruction, and guidance.

7. *Repetition*—Rinse and repeat cycles 1 to 6, over and over again.

8. *The Next Level*—If there is no one readily available in your current life/circle that you desire to learn from, or, more realistically, there is a person you really admire, then cold-contacting a potential mentor can be a fun challenge to pursue. If you work hard enough to hunt down their contact info and reach out in an authentic, relatable, and non-pushy way, then it may spark the mentor-relationship you desire and add valuable, specific instruction into your future endeavors.

AGE IS JUST A NUMBER

Lots of things happen to us in the process of growing older. Typically we grow until we stop, and then we reach the stage of slow decline, as we fight against the natural decline of our body's function, from head to toe. Few things improve over time (wine, wood, etc.), which is where the word "entropy" comes from: "a state of disorder, or a decline into disarray." It takes work to fight against this—real, consistent, energy-expending effort.

One of the positive effects of growing older is wisdom—which is also said to come with age. As with most generalizations, this is true a lot of the time, but the degree that it's true is up to you. The danger in amassing personal knowledge and experience is what follows close behind: the closed-mindedness of pride and ignorance. Knowledge never equates to wisdom. Wisdom involves the proper *application* of knowledge, which shows that it still requires some form of action. And it's not a stagnant state, nor is it a state that can ever be fully attained in this life.

"Ignorance is always correctable. But what shall we do if we take ignorance to be knowledge?"
—Neil Postman

Being a lifelong learner means just that: learning your *whole* life. Even with age, learning shouldn't be replaced, but it does experience a shift. This shift is a transfer of weight from the side of learning to the side of teaching. The more you learn, the more you have a responsibility to help others learn. The older we get, the more we should be sharing and giving of the knowledge we have already received.

However, this does *not* mean that learning is nonexistent in our later years. We must strive for humility, even more so, as we grow older. One of the ways this is commonly missed is in teachability. As mentioned, there is a natural and needed shift throughout our life—from learning to teaching—but there shouldn't be a disappearance or removal of either. The problem is, our teachability is often discarded subconsciously. The more we increase in our experience and knowledge, and the more we teach others what we've learned, the less we will see the need to learn from others (and partly because there are fewer people we can actually learn from).

The older we are, the more we have to personally (and intentionally) initiate the process of others-focused learning. It provides benefit through what we continue to learn, but also through the active reminder to carry a humble spirit throughout each phase of life, both young and old (and every place in between).

Initiating the process entails two main steps:

1. Internal recognition that, despite growth in experience, knowledge, and wisdom, we still don't know it all and there is always something to be learned from others.

2. Approach those who are older and wiser than you (or younger with a different perspective and experience to compare/contrast with), seeking to learn and grow from what they can offer, and helping to cultivate personal humility while strengthening your commitment to the lifelong goal of being a learner.

As we grow in age and wisdom, we begin to value our time, and what's remaining of that time, more and more. Thus, it makes sense for us to be more hesitant in committing our valuable time to teaching others *unless* they are humble and committed to the process. Understanding this perspective can help improve our awareness of how to approach a mentor relationship in a respectful and intentional way.

APPLICATION

Creating and cultivating a spirt of teachability is a worthwhile endeavor. Mentors, tutors, disciplers, coaches, role models—the title isn't as important as the concept shared throughout. Seeking someone to invest in our life and personal growth is viewed as common knowledge—something that is so true that it is acknowledged by all (or, at least a majority).

Personally, I know no greater catalyst for growth and development than the individuals who invested their time and energy into me. I am happily and heartily an outspoken evangelist to the reality of this truth, for all who would listen.

In order for motivation to turn into action, we need to be told why. It's a wise thing to ask, because if we don't start with why, then failure will be looming around the corner. So now that we've seen the context and concept of what teachability entails, let us start with *why*.

WHY WE NEED TO BE TAUGHT BY OTHERS

Humans are more tangible and personable than words.
- Books are great, but they carry a singular dimension. We can learn *a ton* from books, but books can't talk back to us. They can't interact with us, adjusting to our current state in the moment-to-moment emotional sway of daily life. They merely meet us where we are, for better or worse. A book provides us with a perspective that's locked in time, forever set in the trajectory established by the author. *People* meet us in the current time-space continuum in which we reside. It doesn't get more tangible than that.

People help us regain our eye-sight.
- We are often blind to our own biases; we genuinely can't see where our misleading assumptions or irrational beliefs reside. It's common sense to seek a tool that elevates our quality of life.

When our eyesight becomes blurred, we acquire glasses (or contacts) to provide the corrective lens that helps us clearly see the world we live in. This produces greater vibrancy and clarity in all aspects of life. Having others teach us provides us with this tool—a relational "contact lens"—through which we see the world as accurately and as clearly as possible.

People present a real-life intersection (and combination) of the two methods of learning.

- We learn through acquiring knowledge and life experience. When taught by others, we get the best of both worlds. Not only do they teach us knowledge about information and skills, but they also provide real-life experience for us to learn from (secondhand). Furthermore, they can provide the needed feedback to help interpret our firsthand experiences in life, solidifying what those situations and circumstances may teach us.

Uncontested living produces a mediocre mindset and a false confidence in our own legitimacy.

- Confirmation bias is the tendency to interpret whatever we are learning as confirmation of the existing beliefs or theories we already have. This seeps into all we do, including the books, articles, or information we read, as well as the entertainment we consume and the people we converse with. Typically, it entails some form of the same ideas we already ascribe to, making us more secure and safe in our thoughts. Challenging what we believe will only strengthen the beliefs that are important, while revealing the areas of our thinking that contain discrepancies and flaws. So, go get in an argument, but keep it friendly. (Side note: Having convictions and knowing what we believe is a good thing. But we must be cautious of the "intolerance of disagreement" that can develop from a one-sided stream of input.)

A teacher or mentor will be able to meet your situational needs more efficiently and effectively.

- This takes place both from a timing standpoint and from a feedback standpoint. Timing-wise, they are interacting with us in the exact moment of our discussion, versus some written work that's stuck in time (see argument above). But effectiveness is a multiplier that other forms of learning can't even sniff. Having instantaneous feedback on our views and ideas, while interacting with another person, provides an additional layer of usefulness in learning what our tendencies are and how they affect what we learn, for better or worse.

People ask critical and thought-provoking questions.

- Having to think on our feet and answer direct, intentional questions helps to clarify what we truly believe about the ideas floating in our head. It ensures that we do the mental lifting required, taking time to *actually* think about the question and then provide a pertinent answer.

Accountability, accountability, accountability.

- We need it. Nuff said. If we give way to lethargy and laziness in our lives, then following through (in anything) can be a mountainous task. Many times, there are desires and commitments we'd like to keep, but in our own strength we're unable to follow through. Teachers, mentors, or individuals who are investing in our personal lives provide accountability to assist us in staying true to what we say (and know) we want—*especially* when we don't feel like it.

We are designed for teammates.

- With real life being very un-fairy-tale-esque, encouragement can be a dire resource. Having a mentor, coach, or teacher can bring the much-needed slap on the back when the going gets tough. We need instruction, encouragement, affirmation, and tough love to support us in this journey of life. Stop playing solo; find a teammate.

Backs don't need to be broken.

- Burdens can be overbearing, and carrying heavy things takes a toll. With the excessive nature of the load we often bear, having another person for counsel and consolation can alleviate enough of the burden to make it bearable again. It also frees us up to handle or overcome situations with greater confidence, peace, joy, and emotional stability.

IT WORKS BOTH WAYS

Surprisingly, the effects of teachability work in both directions, to both the giver and the receiver.

Intakes and outputs are two different mediums of transportation, but they both involve the flow of information. When we teach others, we end up solidifying information in a new and more tangible way. In order to communicate the knowledge or skill we possess in a way that is understandable and concise, we must be able to take what's inside our mind and make it digestible and knowable by those receiving the input. This is easier said than done, and oftentimes what we think we know is really only clear inside our own head.

But the self-benefits of teaching others don't end there. In fact, you don't even have to end up teaching someone to benefit from the effects of preparing to teach someone. A study published in the *Journal of Memory and Cognition*[1] found that students who were told they would be required to teach the subject matter they were studying had "more complete and better organized free recall" of the material than the students who were studying the material in preparation for being personally tested on it. Maybe we should all pretend to be teachers.

Beyond benefitting from the *process* of teaching, we will inevitably experience growth by interacting with another person's worldview on a personal and regular level, teaching you more about your own worldview and where your biases or self-limiting beliefs lie—not to mention, teaching itself is a *learned* skill. The process of learning never ends, even for teachers.

THE FAR SIDE OF TEACHABILITY

"The art of being wise is the art of knowing what to overlook."
—William James, American psychologist and philosopher

If *learning* (in the process of mastery) is the simplicity, and *teachability* is the complexity, then **discernment** is the simplicity on the far side of complexity.

With our inevitable limitations as human beings, discretion and moderation are important concepts to keep in mind. Just as recovery is a nonnegotiable after physical exertion, so too is the requirement of discernment when living with a spirit of teachability.

---

1   John F. Nestojko, Dung C. Bui, Nate Kornell, Elizabeth Ligon Bjork, "Memory & Cognition," *Journal of Memory and Cognition*, 2014, Vol. 42, No. 7, p. 1038.

Discernment can simply be defined as "the ability to judge well." It means you are able to accurately determine the worth of the information you are receiving. There's no greater need for discernment than in the role of a judge. As a judge, your sole job is to discern who's guilty and who's innocent. Discerning is determining right from wrong *accurately.*

When it comes to learning from others, all voices are created equal, but not all merit the same value. And thus, not all voices should be given equal footing in our own lives.

As we accumulate knowledge and experience, we naturally shift from predominantly learning to predominantly teaching. During this shift, the usefulness of what we are taught by others is reduced. The older (and hopefully wiser) we grow, the more discernment is needed when translating the information we gather into our daily lives. With the bodily decline from age, so too comes the decline in usefulness of things taught by others, in both impact and pertinence.

All of this is to say that while we should never stop learning from others (throughout our *entire* lives), we should be growing in our ability to accurately discern which voices are worth our full attention/reception and which aren't helpful for us to follow.

SOME PRACTICAL IDEAS ON DISCERNMENT

The key to growing in discernment is knowing which voices deserve your *sustained* attention. Here are some observations for this process:

1. **Not all teachers (voices) are created equal.**
    This has already been stated, but it warrants being repeated. In anything that's communicated, the person who is sharing brings a lifetime of experiences that create the context for what they are saying. Hardly ever do we have the full picture, let alone a basic understanding, of what that context is. The more we understand the person, the more we can understand the true meaning behind what they say. Context is key.

2. **Not all information is created equal.**
    Even people who deserve to be listened to will, at times, have thoughts of lesser merit. There will be people we consider "safe"

(in reference to what they know and believe) but, even then, we still must have eyes and ears of discernment when being taught, because no person is infallible.

3. **Not all instruction is pertinent.**
Sometimes what we are being taught is virtuous and helpful but not currently applicable to our lives. With how much information is available today, we must know what to save and what to discard, based on its current usefulness. Situational application is a good lens to help inform our discernment for what we digest.

4. **Everyone has a bias.**
This reality also applies to the individuals who teach us. The deeper our relationship grows, the more we begin to see their true selves and where their inherent biases lie. This is not justification to discredit their tutelage, but rather a reminder for awareness and discernment.

5. **Constant contradiction can cripple.**
If we allow all voices equal footing in our lives, then we will be bombarded with constant, contradictory thoughts. This brings confusion instead of clarity and causes inaction instead of growth. Seek counsel, use discernment, obtain wisdom, and then act.

6. **Confirmation bias is blinding.**
While we shouldn't allow a bombardment of contradictory voices, we should welcome some disagreement and opposition. If we surround ourselves solely with those whom we agree, confirmation bias is allowed free reign in our thoughts and in our lives. Find the balance and live in the tension.

7. **Spoon-feeding breeds dependence.**
Being overly teachable leads to a reliance on others for growth. This swings the pendulum of responsibility fully to the side of the teacher (or mentor) for our personal development. Long-term growth is impossible when it's based entirely on someone that's not you.

8. **We're all human.**
Thus, no one should be granted absolute authority. Mistakes will be made, inaccurate things will be said, and disagreements will be had. There's no escaping human nature.

SUMMATION

> *"Love tells me I am everything. Wisdom tells me I am nothing.*
> *And between those two banks, flows the river of my life."*
> —Nisargadatta, Indian philosopher

And that is why we need others to help us navigate our voyage down the river of life, keeping us from careening into the bank of self-absorption or crashing on the bank of self-abasement.

At the end of the day, teachability requires us to take *ownership*—because we are the ones who have to live with the decisions we make and the actions we take. Our life is just that: *our* life. We can either help ourselves out, or hurt ourselves—knowingly or unknowingly. Learning is not solely a "me"-centered process; it is also an others-centered pursuit. There are millions of people around us who have something to share.

It's time we start listening.

FEAR

"Fear is like fire. It can cook for you. It can heat your house. Or it can burn you down."

—CUS D'AMATO (MIKE TYSON'S TRAINER)

"Action feeds and strengthens confidence; inaction in all forms feeds fear. To fight fear, act. To increase fear—wait, put off, postpone."

—DAVID SCHWARTZ

"Choking is about thinking too much. Panic is about thinking too little."

—MALCOLM GLADWELL

MY STORY

CHILDHOOD FEARS

Fear is a complicated thing.

While I don't remember many specifics from childhood, I do remember being an easily frightened child. I liked to be in control and I liked the safety of my comfort zone—the experiences that were familiar to my personal experience and interpretation of the world. Anything that rocked the boat was to be avoided, shunned, and opposed at all costs. Usually, this meant breaking down into fits of tears, hoping that crying would facilitate my departure from the immediate situation.

The earliest memory I can recall of this form of fear was at a Kansas City Royals baseball game. I was with my parents and sister, and it was a beautiful Friday night. Baseball was a sport I loved as a kid, mainly because it was so accessible. (All that was needed was a glove, a ball, and Dad's approval, and we would head out to the backyard to play some catch or work on batting practice.) As with most Friday night games, the highlight of the night, for the majority of fans attending, was the post-game fireworks show. Let's just say I wasn't a part of the majority.

The loud noises of the fireworks sounded like shotgun blasts reverberating throughout the stadium. Thus ensued my crying defense mechanism to avoid the "unsafe" situation. This was my childhood form of a fear response.

There's another example that comes to mind, and it involves theme parks. What child doesn't love going to Disneyland, World's of Fun, or Six Flags? It is pure adventure and awe—except for one thing: the big, scary, and intimidating roller-coasters. The only ally I had in avoiding this new danger was the height requirement. But, at a certain point, this no longer provided any benefit. Instead, it became an added incentive for those who were pushing me to ride. While I was too young to know it, the phrase "ride or die" had a different meaning to me at the time. In my mind, it was ride *and* die. No way.

And then, as with most others who share this early trepidation, everything changed. When I finally mustered up the courage to take my first ride (or more accurately, my parents worked hard enough to coerce me), I surprisingly loved it! The experience wasn't terrifying—it was *thrilling*. I became like all the other kids who grow out of their fear of roller coasters and become the people we fondly refer to as "coaster-junkies."

How do we grow out of fear? Is it something that operates in parallel fashion to our wardrobe, moving from size to size with each passing year of our childhood? Or is it something that is only changed when experiences or circumstances force us to?

CHANGING FEARS

Something that's "thrilling" refers to an event or action that causes someone to have a sudden feeling of excitement or pleasure. This is the experience of riding a roller-coaster; and after having my eyes opened to it's beauty, I shifted from being a fear avoider to being a thrill seeker.

This trait prevailed throughout my younger years, lasting all the way to the present day. Thrill-seeking is an addictive character trait because of the biological processes at play, with dopamine being its key driver. From adolescence to youth, this key driver undoubtedly played a role in my transition from being a scared safety seeker to being an adventurous thrill seeker.

Hindsight makes it much easier to connect the dots; it's much harder to do in the moment. One telling sign of this transition was my affinity for scary movies. Horror films have zero redemptive value, and it is easy to argue for their uselessness. But what they do provide is *a thrill*. While I didn't recognize it at the time, the thrill is what I sought, and those movies were another means to an end for me.

Other examples include motorcycles, an intense love affair with snowboarding, an affinity for watching any and all extreme sports, new activities and adventures with friends, and competing on as big of a stage as possible in golf. All of these pursuits provided novelty and adventure, giving me the thrill I unknowingly longed for.

But, while I was able to grow out of my childhood fears, fear itself didn't go away. Instead, it rebranded itself under a new alias.

LASTING FEARS

These undercover fears started to resurface during my professional golf career. The thrill of competing turned into the fear of losing. The thrill of challenging my personal abilities and seeing what I could produce turned into the fear of my inability and of the possibility of *not* producing what I was capable of. This is the fear that cripples, and I got a front-row seat to the paralysis that follows.

There were two instances where this reality was seen so clearly, and the culmination of them both came in 2015.

At the beginning of the year I played in a qualifier for the OneAsia Tour. During the first three rounds, I played freely, carelessly, and confidently—a powerful combination on the golf course. This left me in second place with the final round to go. Being in this position was an experience I was largely unfamiliar with as a professional, and the results revealed my novice nature. Throughout the round I got stuck in my head, in the doubts and unknowns, producing in me a controlling, fearful, and uncertain approach that led to lackluster results.

Finishing in tenth place, I knew I wouldn't be getting into many events but there was a chance for a few. This chance turned into competing in five tournaments throughout 2015, beginning in May with the OneAsia GS Caltex Maekyung Open, in Seoul, South Korea.

Here's where fear enters the picture.

A few days before the tournament, I received the official tee times for the first two rounds. Lo and behold, there I was—Thane Marcus Ringler—with the very first tee time on hole #10 in the first round. Not only was I in the first tee time, but I was also the first one to tee off in the group. In my first international event as a professional, I would be kicking off the entire tournament with the opening tee shot. Yes, I'll admit it: I was intimidated.

With my nerves strung out and my palms sweaty, I stepped up to the tee trying to have my mind sit still for even a second so that I could focus on the task at hand. All the preparation and work of my lifelong career had led me to this moment, and what would I do? How would I respond? Would it be greatness? Or would it be embarrassment and failure?

With heart pounding, I stepped up to the ball and hit one of the *worst* opening drives imaginable—a 30-yard block, pushed so far right it had a 0 percent chance of staying in-bounds. And with that, I kicked off a yearlong battle, experiencing the fruit of my fears firsthand, and fighting as hard as I could to not let them take ownership of me and my career.

This was no short battle. In fact, the heat of the battle came later that fall in November.

The week before the biggest tournament of my professional career—The Australian Open—I played in a small mini-tour event to sharpen my competitive mindset and my game. During my warmup for the third round of the event, fear decided to launch a full-on attack, in the form of the dreaded "yips."

For those who aren't familiar with the yips, they are involuntary movements/spasms that interfere with the desired execution of a skill or movement. Simply put, you can't hit the shot you want to hit, and it is directly (if not entirely) a result of fear taking over your mind. Once fear takes the reigns of your mind, your body is left with no choice but to follow.

While often associated with putting, the yips came for me with my wedges—specifically, any wedge from a distance of 20 yards up to 130 yards. These are the "scoring" clubs, the shots that are supposed to be your greatest weapon as a professional—the best tool for making birdies and winning tournaments. And now they became my greatest enemy. This mental inhibition of fear led to my worst round as a professional golfer (shooting 87) a week before the most important tournament I had played in up to this point. Fear ran rampant.

From a mental standpoint, the following week was the greatest fight of my life. I had to go from a mental state of rock bottom, to regaining the confidence needed to compete with the likes of Jordan Spieth, Adam Scott, and Lee Westwood. Talk about moving mountains. This task felt like one of those insurmountable feats.

CONCEPT

So, what do you do? How do you fight fear off? How do you keep fear from controlling your thoughts, beliefs, and actions? How do you go from slave to victor? How do you move from being used/controlled by fear that hurts you to using and controlling that same fear to help you?

These are questions that don't come with easy answers. But those questions are the most important ones to ask and, more important, to seek answers to.

Before we talk about some ideas on what those answers are, we need to first build a foundation for understanding what fear is and what its role or creational purpose entails.

UNIVERSAL UNDERPINNINGS

Is fear universal? Another way to ask the same question is this: does every human face fear at some level? The answer is assuredly *yes*.

Fear is as inescapable as the taxes you pay (or even the waste you excrete). This parallel is seen on two different fronts because, with both fear and taxes, there are ways to work around the system. More on that to come.

We can confidently conclude that we've been created with a natural fear response. This is embedded in in our peripheral nervous system. Within this portion of our nervous system, there lie two segments: the autonomic nervous system and the somatic nervous system. A major function of the autonomic nervous system is the involuntary responses that help regulate our physiological functions in light of the circumstantial needs.

This autonomic nervous system is further broken down into two categories: the sympathetic nervous system and the parasympathetic nervous system. The most common way to describe these two systems is "fight or flight" (sympathetic nervous system) and "rest and digest" (parasympathetic nervous system). Both are essential to survival. One meets the immediate need of the situation or stressor, whereas the other facilitates the needed recovery after the heightened response.

Within these systems, one of the physiological processes at play is our fear response, and its purpose is to preserve our life in the face of danger. Each physiological effect serves a role in furthering our life preservation. The heart rate speeds up, which drives more blood through the body, carrying the extra oxygen and glucose (fuel) needed to withstand a threat. Blood vessels constrict in order to retain core body heat and to increase the vascular resistance, preserving the loss of blood in the case of an injury. Our pupils dilate as a natural response to heightened focus and the processing of important information. Our digestive system slows down in order to preserve the nutrition and substance we gain from the fuel, while removing distraction of the needed discharges associated with the process.

This is a small list of all that the body does on a daily basis to keep up with the ever-changing demands of human life. It is remarkable and miraculous to see and understand all the ways our bodies adapt to enable us not only to survive but also to thrive.

THE PURPOSE OF FEAR

It's clear to see that we have been made with a healthy dose of fear—for the purpose of keeping us alive and well. It's the response that automatically kicks in during situations akin to a poisonous snake slithering your way or taking one step too close in straining to peer over the ledge of a cliff. We have all personally experienced the 20-inch-subwoofer pounding of our heart in those moments.

This shows us that, at its core, fear is a good, healthy, and beneficial part of our bodies and the preservation of life. It is an internal mechanism of survival, the response of our body to any stimulus of danger we come across.

Yet sometimes, the intent or purpose of a bodily function can be compromised. These include both situational and systemic compromises. Situationally, our fear functions are compromised when we place false or illogical value to things that don't deserve it. Systemically, we create cyclical fear loops from the experiences encountered throughout our lives, but many times during the most malleable period of life—our childhood.

One pervasive aspect of fear is the concept of *control*. When control of our life is in jeopardy, fear is the innate response that kicks our autonomic nervous system into action. This response is commonly shared by both healthy and unhealthy fear. Sometimes a bad work review or bad exam score can be all that's needed to jumpstart the nervous system into a fight or flight state. These situations, where control is taken out of our hands—to the greater degree of life and death, as well as the lesser degree of pass or fail—are affectionately known as *stress*.

One of society's most commonly used self-descriptions is: "stressed out". Literally, this can be translated as: being in a state where stress has maximized, or overwhelmed, your ability to effectively cope and properly adapt to the stressor with the needed physiological responses. "Stress" is not a word that would be universally agreed upon as synonymous to fear, but they produce a parallel response and a synonymous result.

The point in comparing fear and stress is to show that, with repeated use and abuse, we progressively lose the benefit of our body's natural response to these "threatening" situations. And that reveals the physical problem with fear. When we leave the realm of healthy fears and move into the realm of unhealthy fears, we begin to compromise what was intended for our good, turning it into a response that methodically degrades both our health and our sanity.

THE DARK SIDE OF FEAR

The picture painted so far shows that the primary creational role of fear is this: a natural response to a threatening situation, meant to protect us from harm that might result in the expiration of life. But, like most good things in life, it can be corrupted into a harmful response. What was designed to protect us can turn into the very thing that damages us. This is the unhealthy version of fear, the fear that resides on the dark side.

At the core of unhealthy fear lies a loss of reality. It is the shift from seeing with an objective lens to seeing with a subjective lens. It's a transition from logical fear to *irrational* fear.

Irrationality encapsulates all forms of unhealthy fear. It is a fear that is not logical or reasonable. It is viewing a situation as a life-threatening scenario, even if it's as physically harmless as speaking in front of an audience. And so often, when exposed for the light to shine on them, our fears are as silly as they sound. Yet rarely do we ever shed a light on the irrational ways we subject our bodies to the stress adaptation that is, day by day, eroding the health and integrity of our body's ability to adapt while simultaneously reducing our personal (and professional) capabilities.

This is the ultimate problem with irrational fear. Beyond the physical ramifications, it has devastating effects on our ability to reach our full potential.

IRRATIONALITY IS NOT THE EXCEPTION

Irrational fears are much more common and pervasive than we would like to admit.

Take, for instance, the fear of man. This is a fear known by all but admitted by few. It is the fear that says "I don't want to/won't do X or Y because of what this person or that individual will think." This could be a fear of singing in public, or the fear of making mistakes (perfectionism), or the fear of tripping when walking on stage, or the fear of dancing when someone could be watching; all of these fears stem from a fear of man/woman—and more specifically, a fear of what he or she will think of you in the case that something embarrassing happens. Hence, you are now deriving a portion of your purpose and value in life from some other human being, which places greater worth in that person than they deserve.

We all fall prey to these illogical fears. The exception is found in those who recognize where their irrational fears lie. And beyond recognition, they are able to develop the practice of facing and overcoming those fears in the situations when the body should not be subjected to the fear response.

The question that usually follows is whether this is a natural/innate propensity or something that's developed throughout life. As per usual, the answer is—*yes*. There are very real differences in each person's capacity for fear. But, the largest component of those propensities results from what we have been exposed to throughout our lives, the experiences that so often inform and create the idea of what "deserves" to be feared.

A pertinent illustration of our differing capacities can be seen in the arena of war. No one describes this more poignantly than Col. David Hackworth, reminiscing on his time in the Korean War. He said, "When you're fighting, you're scared. And it's such an all pervasive sort of fear that you can't even pinpoint what the feeling is… And that's what bravery is. It's not *fearlessness*; it's the ability to get off your ass and charge even when your mouth is dry, your gut is tight, and your brain is screaming *Stay down!* But even the bravest of men have a breaking point."

He went on to reach this conclusion: "man is like a bottle. On the battlefield, fear is what fills him up and fuels him to perform. But some bottles are smaller than others. When a guy becomes unglued during a firefight, it's just that his bottle has filled up and overflowed; it's time for him to get away and let the fear drain out. But even when it does, there is a catch: from that moment on, the man is like a spent cartridge, and no amount of gunpowder will ever make him a real fighter again" (*About Face*, p.76).

This is a helpful picture of the reality that we all have differing fear capacities, depicted here as different sizes of bottles that can hold different amounts of fear. But more times than not, we use this understanding as justification instead of clarification. We turn the possibility into surety and make it the premise for our personal credo of laziness and security.

The problem lies not in our differing capacities but in our shared irrationality.

FROM SEEDS TO DEEP-ROOTED TREES

Every deep-rooted conviction begins with the planting of a seed of an idea. Over time, with the nurturing of sunlight and water (stimulants), growth occurs. Something that began as a very small oval can end up growing into a massive tree, withstanding the fiercest assaults from extreme conditions or climates.

For most Americans like me (growing up in a peaceful and prosperous nation), the majority of fears we harbor as adults were formed from our childhood. Here are four examples to illustrate this reality:

Potential Path #1: Results Driven

If as a child, you are told that self-worth (your individual value) is derived from results and accomplishments, then you will do whatever it takes to get good grades, or win the gold medal, or have a competitive advantage in fill-in-the-blank activity. As you continue to build this belief system, you begin to refine your activities, leaving only the things you know you're the best at doing—the things in your wheelhouse.

This creates a heightened value of security and comfort above, and in the place of, growth. As you continue on into college and beyond, you consistently choose to stick with the endeavors within your comfort zone, a zone that increasingly narrows in its scope.

The fruit from the initial seed of values is a tree of fear and doubt that restricts and reduces your capacity, limiting your potential to your unique skillset. Taken to the extreme, you slowly become incapable of any task that sits outside of your specific skill set and, more important, your beloved *comfort zone.*

Potential Path #2: People Driven

Maybe you were likable as a kid. You were the baby everyone couldn't stop holding, the infant everyone wanted to babysit, the toddler who mirrored an angel, the elementary-school kid who seemed to be naturally gifted at everything. As a result, you became very popular in high school and were a social flower seen in full bloom.

With living a praised life, you began to find your value and personal worth in what others thought of you, marking the beginning of a life based on impressing others. It influenced the choice you made for college, the career path you chose after graduating, the company you applied to work for, the clothes you now wear, the people you call your friends, and on and on.

This life based on appearance is a life that is enslaved to the fear of man/woman. You base your decisions on what he/she will think of you, and any personal conviction or belief you once had is now subjected to the opinion of others. There is no freedom in this tree of fear, just servitude to the desires of others and a deep-seated fear of living life authentically, genuinely, and *fearlessly*.

Potential Path #3: Worthlessness Driven

As a kid, you may have been told you were worthless, that you were incapable of anything of merit, and that your life was destined for doom and destruction, never to amount to anything of importance. As a result, you never gave much effort or energy into school, to furthering your own learning or abilities. In everything you did, you choose the path of least resistance and never tried anything beyond your current capacity.

This led to a systemic lack of belief in yourself. The message from your childhood was deeply implanted in your conscious and subconscious alike. You have ended up living just to live, pursuing pleasure when available mainly because you have nothing else to derive any semblance of happiness or purpose from.

This tree of fear is one rooted in your own inability. It is the fear that tells you that trying isn't worth it, that your life has no greater meaning than to simply be lived, that there is nothing of importance other than the small moments of happiness occasionally found but never sustained. On its face, it is the fear of doing something hard or challenging, beyond your current self—striving for the place you *could* be but currently aren't. This fear will forever keep you in stagnancy and mediocrity. Your life has become a self-fulfilling prophecy.

Potential Path #4: Security Driven

Maybe you were raised being told to value safety and security above all else. You started a penny bank when you were three years old, and have been establishing a blanket of security ever since. As you grew through the stages of childhood, you began to gravitate towards what you were best at. You made sure that you were on the path of dependability instead of on the path of your greatest interest/passion.

A commitment to remaining in your safety net led you to a respected college where you were guaranteed to be accepted, which puts you on the path of a generally accepted career, providing longevity and lots of safety. This produced a job after college with the same type of credentials: safety and security.

After some time working in this position, you have come to realize that there is nothing fulfilling about the job in and of itself, other than safety. Yet, you ignore what your heart is telling you to do and what you know you truly want to do, simply because you can't handle the risk. Risk is a four-letter word of worse implications than any other vice that may leave your lips. Death seems more comfortable than leaving the comfort and security of your safety-net life.

INVISIBLE FORCES AT PLAY

As with any story, there are countless more that haven't been told. No single illustration can show the full story, just a snippet. But those snippets illustrate the power of the seeds planted in our youth. More times than not, these seeds leave a lasting impact that will rarely, if ever, be discovered by their carriers or purveyors—us.

One of the most powerful components in these stories is the underlying and invisible forces at play. Human beings are all wired in a similar fashion, and because of this, we have internal mechanisms that are more automatic than we'd like to admit. When certain individuals become cognizant of these mechanisms, they can use that knowledge to exploit others (unbeknownst to them) for their own benefit.

This is insightfully depicted in Robert Cialdini's book *Influence: The Psychology of Persuasion*. One of the most powerful tendencies we unknowingly possess is our adamant desire for *consistency*. Above most everything in life, we want to be consistent with what we say/do, so much so that we will resort to irrationality before inconsistency.

Speaking on commitment and consistency, Cialdini writes, "[T]his weapon of influence lies deep within us, directing our actions with quiet power. It is, quite simply, our nearly obsessive desire to be (and to appear) consistent with what we have already done. Once we have made a choice or taken a stand, we will encounter personal and interpersonal pressures to behave consistently with that commitment. Those pressures will cause us to respond in ways that justify our earlier decision" (*Influence: The Psychology of Persuasion*, p. 57).

He goes on to say, "[W]e all fool ourselves from time to time in order to keep our thoughts and beliefs consistent with what we have already done or decided" (p. 59).

So, what's the point? Why does it matter?

"To understand why consistency is so powerful a motive, it is important to recognize that in most circumstances consistency is valued and adaptive. Inconsistency is commonly thought to be an undesirable personality trait. The person whose beliefs, words, and deeds don't match may be seen as indecisive, confused, and two-faced, or even mentally ill. On the other side, a high degree of consistency is normally associated with personal and intellectual strength. It is at the heart of logic, rationality, stability, and honesty" (p. 60).

When fear loops are created in our childhood, consistency can change from our ally to our enemy. This consistency bias inhibits our ability to change and our liberation from fear's menacing grip.

By simply knowing—becoming aware of—these tendencies, we can be liberated and assisted in the fight to overcome our self-created irrational beliefs and fears. When we've operated under these influences for a long period of time, everything within us will scream once we begin to operate "inconsistently." But this does **not** mean that it is the wrong thing to do. There are many times or situations in life when our emotions betray us and cannot be trusted. In these moments, consistency is often the one to blame.

A PLEA FOR FULFILLMENT

The next logical question is, does facing your fears need to be a habit formed by everyone? Of course not. Needs are different from wants. I want everyone to face their fears and see the benefit in overcoming their own limitations, but what I want and what you want are two different realities. Ultimately, each person has both basic needs (food, water, sleep) and personal needs (family, freedom, house, income, relationships, etc.), and both of these needs trump the specific need for facing fears.

A better question to ask is, would everyone benefit from incorporating this habit into their lives? Yes!

To put it simply, irrational fear reduces our ability to produce our best and truest work, which, in turn, reduces the benefit and service we are able to provide for others in our world and in our life. Beyond that, it keeps us from experiencing the deepest and richest fulfillment and joy that comes from contributing to society in an unimpeded and unrestrained way.

If you're asking yourself, *Is it worth it? Am I called to a life of striving to live fearlessly?* The answer you need to accept is this: since you're reading this book, yes! Jesus said it best: "To whom much is given, much is required" (Luke 12:48).

APPLICATION

Now that the theory of fear, a base foundation, has been laid, we must move on to the work of applying this knowledge to our everyday lives.

The following ideas stem directly from my own experience in fighting to overcome the crippling fears I faced during my professional golf career, which limited my ability to perform at my best. My fears kept me from producing the results I was capable of, and they were all highly illogical and irrational. But, as we've already seen, just because they're irrational doesn't mean we will see them as that, let alone conquer them. Fighting for change is just that: a fight.

If we are to overcome the menacing obstacle of fear, then we need to know the tools, tricks, techniques, and strategies that can help us gain liberation. But before we get there, let's look at the path of overcoming fear.

THE PATH OF LEANING INTO FEAR

This is a picture of the road traveled, the one that leads to our becoming a fear conquerer:

1. **Recognize it.** You must *first* become aware of the fear in order to beat the fear. If you never recognize its presence, then there will be no way to address it. Growth begins with an acceptance of reality before there can be progress toward a better reality.

2. **Discover the lie.** Irrational fear's power rests in your belief of the lie it proclaims. This means that you must first unearth the lie that's embedded within your fear so that you can see what *isn't* truthful about its claims.

3. **Replace it with truth.** A lie is not easily let go of. Just because we know something isn't true doesn't mean we want to let go of our belief in it. Letting go is uncomfortable, difficult, strenuous, and scary. This is where we must become "personal pastors"— preaching the truth to ourselves (in love). As the saying goes, "the truth will set you free."

4. **Reprogram your brain.** Being used to operating on a lie, your brain will need a systems overhaul in order to be able to run off of truth instead of lies. This is where the blood, sweat, and tears come in. It takes *work.* And work you must give, *daily.* At first, it will seem as if you are making little to no progress, but with persistence and repeated effort, progress will be made and you will begin to gain ground, reestablishing control over your fear and your life.

5. **Habitualize the process.** Repeating this cycle for any and all areas of fear in your life will transform who you are and what you're able to do in life. Living a life of facing your fears will result in the freedom to explore the ends of your personal limitations, reaching for what's beyond them. It means that you are actively looking for the areas of discomfort in order to meet, sit down, and begin to form a friendship with the discomfort. Slowly but surely you will drop the prefix and transform that discomfort into comfort.

HOW TO STOP FEEDING FEAR

In order to remove fear from our daily lives, we must stop feeding it. In order to stop feeding it, we must know what fuels fear. Recognition always precedes proper action, and that's what this is for—helping us help ourselves.

So, here we go:

- *Irrational thoughts and beliefs*—This one has already been covered extensively, so you get the picture. Fear loves crafting a false narrative for us to latch onto and not let go of. It's time we let go and stop feeding fear what it wants.

- *(Future) Uncertainty*—Any sort of uncertainty will likely produce some level of anxiety. The wrong response is to let the uncertainty cripple us and keep us from moving forward. We must live courageously *especially* in the midst of uncertainty.

- *Worries/Anxiety*—Worrying is one of the most useless things we can do. It accomplishes nothing. Yet it does accomplish one thing: it fuels fear. Anxiety and stress have become synonymous phrases, and both of them suck us into a life under the reign of fear.

- *Doubts (usually self-doubt)*—This is one of fear's many mistresses. Doubting our own ability always produces a self-fulfilling prophecy. It's not our lack of ability but our lack of belief in our ability that is the issue. And fear loves capitalizing on our failure to believe.

- *Negative thoughts*—Negativity serves no positive purpose. This is common sense when seen in a sentence but is much harder to accept when life sucker-punches us in the gut. Our thoughts are entirely controlled by ourself, so we need to take ownership and refuse to allow negativity to invade our system—because fear will shortly follow.

- *Helplessness/Hopelessness*—As mentioned earlier, fear stems from a lack of control. When we have no control and no one to help us, helplessness washes over us like a flood. And so too does an all-pervasive fear that overwhelms all parts of our life.

Helplessness is sometimes out of our control, but hopelessness remains our own doing. We must fight for hope, even in the face of helplessness, knowing that fear is lurking at the door to take hold of the reigns of our life.

- *Pressure*—Nothing reveals our true character more than pressure. It raises the stakes and always brings along its close compadre: fear. We must recognize that pressure is ultimately self-inflicted. Even though circumstances create the arena for pressure, we are the ones who create the fear associated with it. We shouldn't run away from pressure but instead enjoy and embrace it as your friend, eliminating any room for fear to join the party.

- *Potential of loss*—This entails any type of loss. It could be monetary, physical, relational, social, appearance, status, identity, etc. Anytime there is a potential of losing something we value in life, fear immediately takes hold of the remote. It begins dictating our thoughts, emotions, and actions. And that is not a helpful or healthy place to be. We must not allow fear to take ownership of us through our possessions (or lack thereof).

- *Momentum*—This could also be called negative momentum or energy. When things are going wrong, they seem to keep getting worse and worse. It's the domino effect, one toppling another until the whole stack is lying on the ground. We must not allow fear to use momentum to take over more and more areas of our mind and heart. When the going gets tough, the tough get going. So, we need to man-up and stop fear in its tracks.

- *Impatience*—Usually when fear shows up on the scene, part of our fight-or-flight response is to increase the speed at which we are operating. This often results in impatience when things continue to not go our way. And the result of impatience is an increase in the presence of fear looming in the shadows. We must remain patient and levelheaded so as not to give fear any hold or footing in the work at hand, no matter how frustrated or impatient we want to be.

- *Loss of perspective*—This happens all the time and is another form of irrationality. Oftentimes it comes from being trapped in our own mind for too long, a place that will always produce a subjective view of how our life is transpiring in the world at large. Perspective must come from those around us and outside our mind so that we can inform our mind of reality and produce a clear lens through which we view our life and the world.

- *Exposure*—The more people watching our actions or performance, the more fear strives to take control. This is a product of our own doing. We must realize that, in these moments, we allow ourselves to fall prey to unnecessary self-monitoring. When we resort to becoming self-consciousness, we open the door for fear and become slaves to what those who are watching think.

- *Lack of exposure*—Conversely, fear wants us to strive for a lack of exposure. This is partly because of the "rational" logic that says that exposure is scary because people may think poorly of us when we receive too much exposure, but even more so because keeping thoughts, doubts, and insecurities to ourself helps sustain the damaging effect of fear. Exposing our fears and shedding light on the darkness allows us to gain control over them. We don't have to live in subjection to our fears. We need to take ownership today and expose them to the light.

- *Comfort/Security*—This has been discussed at length, but it is safe to say that fear loves our preference for security. The more comfortable we become, the more uncomfortable we become with leaving that comfort. Security breeds insecurity, and that's what fear wants.

- *New environments/experiences*—Anything new will inherently have a threshold of discomfort with it. And *that* is exactly why we should embrace the life habit of trying new things. It is an automatic attack on fear. We must embrace new experiences, not run away from them. Fear wants us to hate them, but we need to love them.

- *Bad habits*—Every bad habit in life breeds additional bad habits. Birds of a feather flock together, and bad habits encourage the formation of further bad habits. Fear loves our bad habits because it festers more room and allowance for fear to run rampant in our lives. Eliminating bad habits helps us eliminate fear.

And the best way to do that is by replacing them with good habits.

- *Pessimistic outlook on life*—This runs parallel to negativity mentioned above, but is a nuance worth mentioning. Our outlook on life is self-determined. There is no good reason to be a pessimist. It is rooted in a selfish mindset that tricks us into thinking that living pessimistically is better for us. How irrational. The reality is that optimism will produce more joy, fulfillment, and happiness—and not only for us but also for everyone else in our lives. We need to stop feeding fear what it wants.

- *Self-focus*—Anytime we live selfishly, with ourself being at the center of the universe, fear will have a footing in our life. Life never meets our personal expectations because life isn't about us. But when our eyes are focused solely on ourself, the letdowns of life lay the path for fear to invade our heart and mind.

- *Low self-esteem*—Anytime we have low self-confidence, we are living a life of fear. Fear tells us that we are incapable of anything beyond our current place in life. Fear tells us that we aren't of worth. Fear tells us that others will always be better at X, Y, or Z. We must change the way we look at ourself and, in turn, the way we see fear.

- *Emotion-driven life*—Feelings are a blessing, but they can also be a curse. When we allow our emotions to direct our thoughts, choices, and actions in life, we are setting the stage for a tumultuous ride and the inevitable appearance of fear. We need to live under the direction of our mind, and use our emotions to help our path forward.

- *Lack of foundation*—When we live with no foundation, no why, no greater purpose, fear is licking its chops. Having a greater purpose allows the smaller moments in life to all be connected and helps us maintain the 10,000-foot perpective of day-to-day life. Fear loves when we live based on the moment and not on our purpose. We need to reconnect to our foundation to provide a sturdy base for the attacking storms of fear.

- *Death*—This is the inescapable reality of each human's life. It is the bookend that comes on an unknown future date. We should strive to live under the reality of death but not under the fear of death. When we live under the fear of death, we remove the joy of life and allow a certain level of fear to always be present in our lives. If we knew the day of our death, how differently would we live? There's no reason to wait; we need to start now.

Many of these fuels have similarities, but noting the different names associated with fear can help us deface it and allow us to start living fearlessly amidst the inescapable uncertainties of life.

When you read through the list, I'm sure there were a few that grabbed your attention. The one you struggle with most probably hit you and your subconscious in some way—convicting you of what you know to be true in your heart. The goal is to recognize which specific area is your weakness, focus on increasing your awareness of when it occurs, and then develop a game plan to counteract the fear fuel when it arises.

HOW TO FIGHT

In controlling and conquering fear, there are two realms where the majority of fighting takes place: the mind and the body.

1. The Mind

The mind is where most of the battles take place. The list of fear's fuel almost entirely involves the way we think about it in our mind. It's time we take back control of our minds from fear's suffocating grip.

Here are some ways to do just that:

- *Shift perspective—*
  - o In every situation, we control our view of it. We can be pessimistic or optimistic. We can find things to be grateful for or we can be discontent. We can choose how to respond to a stimulus or we can react—allowing the stimulus to dictate our response. Shifting perspective means we rebrand, repackage, and repurpose situations, enabling our response to be helpful instead of hurtful. This eliminates fear when we begin to see the opportunity for what it is: an opportunity for something good, regardless of whether we like it or not.

- *View all humans equally—*

  o Since the fear of man/woman is such a pervasive root cause, we need to attack this fear with the understanding that all humans are created equal. Whether you're a person who's known as a Hollywood celebrity or a person who is known for living on the street—when everything in life is stripped away, our core worth is equal as human beings. So often we distort this equality through the titles we assign to people. When we call someone a celebrity, we elevate them to an exalted position beyond what they deserve. Likewise, when we call someone a homeless person, we lower them to a position below being human, which is equally undeserved. If we can view each person as a human being, then we will begin to reduce the excessive value placed on their exalted opinion. This helps remove our fear of their thoughts and opinions, beyond having a healthy respect.

- *Sit with it—*

  o Finding comfort in discomfort takes some getting used to. Becoming comfortable in any situation takes time and experience. Michael Jordan was able to hit as many game-winning shots as he did because of all the game-winning shots he missed in order to gain the experience needed to execute when it mattered most. This is similarly true for discomfort. It will be uncomfortable and you won't like it. But with time, patience, and repetition, you too can become comfortable in the discomfort. Find ways to expose yourself to fears and then sit down and listen to them. Have a conversation. Learn what the fear wants and then turn that fear into your friend and helper.

- *Visualize the worst-case scenario—*

  o Worrying about the future is an unhelpful habit, but it can be used for good. When we are fearful of a potential future outcome, a helpful habit is to visualize the worst possible scenario. Once visualized, play out the scenario to its furthest logical outcome/conclusion. This helps us understand what, realistically, could occur if everything possible went horribly wrong. What you will find is that it's never as scary or as frightening as you expect. This process helps us return to the present moment better informed of the reality we face and less fearful of the future, because we know we'll be able to handle it—even if it goes south.

- *Change your self-narrative—*
    - o Self-narrative is a powerful part of life. We can see its power depicted through the illustration of different childhood paths, showing how fear moves from seeds to deep-rooted trees throughout our life. So often we are the ones who implant our own self-narrative to daily life, a narrative that brings with it baggage and self-inflicted insecurities. Who you tell yourself you are tends to be who you live as and who you become. So, in order to live fearlessly, we need to tell ourselves that we are fearless, not in a self-delusional sense, but in a self-instructional way. We need to tell ourselves that we no longer have to fall prey to the limitations fear places on us. Change your self-narrative and remove the implanted seeds of fear in order to live free.

- *Use support—*
    - o Accountability is helpful in every area of life. In facing fears, it is virtually a requirement. A key part of overcoming fear is exposing it. Exposing fear is only possible when there is another person to expose it to. Thus, shedding light on fear requires us to use the support of other people in our life. In order to gain power over fear, add accountability to help you stay true to your new lifestyle, free of fear.

- *Habitualize—*
    - o Facing fears is a lifestyle. It's a developed habit that requires the combination of time and effort. We have to put in the work needed to habitually face and overcome our fears, and we must put in that work over an extended period of time in order to make it last. There's simply no other way.

- *Value courage—*
    - o This is an important aspect of this whole concept. Courage can be defined as the ability to do something that frightens

you. It is strength in the face of pain, or grief, or distress. And it is essential to living a life committed to facing your fears. Not only is it essential, but also it's synonymous. Facing your fears can simply be stated as "living courageously." To live courageously, we must see the value of it—and not only see it but also *believe* in it.

2. The Body

There are very real battles that take place in our body when faced with fear. As we learned earlier, the autonomic nervous system jump-starts a slew of bodily responses to any situation that is categorized as dangerous (whether it truly is or not). Situational awareness of this bodily response is important, but we must also focus on responding appropriately so that we don't fall prey to fear's effect on our body.

The Basics—There are essential components to living a healthy life, and these are the fundamentals needed to counteract the body's natural stress response that so often arises in situations it shouldn't.

- *Eat well—*
  - o Your diet isn't everything, but it is inevitably a factor in how your body functions. As so often is the case, we are either helping or hurting ourselves in how we eat. If we strive toward a healthy, proportionate, nutritional, and balanced diet, we will counteract much of the fuel our body uses to over-activate our own stress response, especially in situations where it isn't needed.

- *Sleep well—*
  - o Sleep is a nonnegotiable. We simply cannot function without it (at least not for very long). But sleep itself is not enough for optimal living. We must strive for quality sleep—both in length and depth. If we are not achieving deep sleep or sleeping for an adequate amount of time, our body will slowly deteriorate by not receiving the recovery time it needs. Thus, the body begins operating on additives, which includes the stress response. Burning the midnight oil is a practice ripe for our body's stress response, a practice that produces a body best known as "stressed out."

- *Exercise—*

  o Fitness is not an essential ingredient to life, but it is an essential ingredient to longevity and productivity. Usefulness diminishes as our bodies' capacity falters. Exercise enables our bodies to perform at higher levels beyond mere stagnancy. It also jump-starts a host of beneficial internal stress responses that are needed—the good kind of stress response resulting from physical exertion, not from fear and anxiety.

The Extras—As with any aspect in life, there are countless tools and techniques we can incorporate to help produce the desired results. Here are three of the most beneficial practices for facilitating a healthy and sustainable level of stress in the body.

- *Breathing—*

  o Breathing is something we do continually and repeatedly, each and every day. Yet rarely are we ever conscious of it. Breathing exercises serve several important functions. First, they teach us to be conscious of our breath. Second, they enable us to work on diaphragm breathing (belly breathing) versus the common chest breathing. Finally, it allows us a level of control over our autonomic nervous system that was previously thought of as scientifically impossible. It is one of the least sexy but most useful tools we have in controlling our stress response. So let's get to work and start breathing, *consciously*.

- *Meditation—*

  o This is a tool that goes hand in hand with breathing. Meditation can look like a lot of things. Each form or style of meditation will include some aspect of the following components: (1) space, (2) quiet, and (3) stillness (and breathing is usually a part of this as well). Meditation helps us become comfortable in the silence of life and helps us gain control of our minds and our thoughts. It can be viewed as the practice of mental discipline, and it is vital to controlling how our bodies react and respond to all that life throws at us.

- *Body knowledge/awareness—*
  - o The more we learn about the body, the more we can know how it functions and operates. Combine that knowledge with the experience of living and that is how we gain a tangible understanding of our own bodies. The key in combining knowledge with experience (and vice versa) is *awareness*. We must develop the habit of living in daily awareness of what our body is telling us. In order to hear, we must first listen. And in order to listen well, we must first know what to be listening for. When we begin to understand more of what our body tells us, we can situationally pivot in the right direction to facilitate the proper response, both for the health and the performance of our body.

THE FAR SIDE OF FEAR

"Life shrinks or expands in proportion to one's courage."
—Anais Nin

As with any area of expertise, mastering fear moves beyond simply overcoming it. Mastery results in using fear to work *for* us instead of *against* us—returning fear to its natural and intended role.

As we saw in the beginning of this chapter, we are internally wired with fear that is created for our benefit. Once we get past the ways we have corrupted our fear response into something that harms us, we can renew a healthy relationship with fear and begin learning how to use our fear response to our advantage.

This practice is commonly (and lovingly) referred to as "flow"—aka being "in the zone." It is a state in which the reality and presence of fear become our allies by harnessing the way our body naturally responds in these scenarios to produce "hyper-focus," enabling us to achieve super-human feats, and accomplish the seemingly impossible. Any successful professional athlete has experienced this on some level. It is the most desired and coveted state by all high-performers, athlete or not. (For a more in-depth analysis of flow, be sure to check out *The Rise of Superman* by Steven Kotler.)

Laurence Gomez also speaks to this state in his book titled *Deep Survival*. He says, "It's not a lack of fear that separates elite performers from the rest of us. They're afraid, too, but they're not overwhelmed by it. They manage fear. They use it to focus on taking correct action."

Whether or not we are able to tap into the power fear can bring, we can all start by recognizing where our irrational fears lie and then do the work to reprogram our mind to reframe our perspective in order to live life free of fear's bondage.

Are you up for the task?

"Action feeds and strengthens confidence; inaction in all forms feeds fear. To fight fear, act. To increase fear—wait, put off, postpone."
—David Schwartz

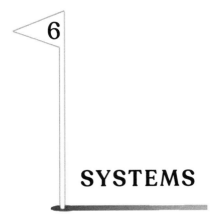

SYSTEMS

"Goals are good for planning your progress and systems are good for actually making progress."

—JAMES CLEAR

"You must bring to your work constancy which keeps steadily at the task; patience which bears difficulties well; and perseverance which prevents the will from flagging."

—A.G. SERTILLANGES

"Hope is rarely enough."

—RYAN HOLIDAY

MY STORY

DEEP DIVE

Systems never mattered to me when I was a kid. Golf was a game and games were meant to be played. And by golly, I was going to play it!

As a child, when you play a game you aren't worried about playing it "the right way," or making it look like everyone else, or focusing on the right form or technique in every movement and pattern you ingrain. You play it because you love it and because it brings you joy. An even more important component for me was having an arena in which to compete.

Taking a dive into the deep end of the pool has its consequences, especially if we're not ready for it. But are we ever fully ready for that first dive? Theorizing or conceptualizing can only do so much good before we simply have to learn by doing.

The first deep dive I took in life was when I entered into collegiate golf. Suddenly, I found myself in a sea of new information and endless complexities, shaping and influencing the final product of my results. Early on, learning wasn't as much of a focus, as I was concerned with simply *not drowning*. In entering this phase of the complexity cycle, I found myself looking to others more than ever before. While teachability is important, copying others is *not* a recipe for success.

My collegiate coach, Coach Jason, was very intentional in building and prescribing systems for our team to implement, to give us the best chance for success. Coming in with hardly any personal systems of my own (in regards to golf), this was immensely helpful. Yet, even in the midst of this process, I found myself looking to other players and different aspects of their game or how they played in order to try to find new elements that would help me be even better. This was a dangerous and deadly habit, but I had very little knowledge that what I was opening took after Pandora's box. Shutting it would be a whole 'nother endeavor.

LEARNING AGAIN

Entering into the professional ranks, this others-focused vision started to increasingly hinder my ability to play my best golf.

During the first year and a half of playing professionally, I subconsciously viewed every round as an opportunity to learn from the other pros I was playing with—all in the hopes of finding that one component, tool, or trick that would set me off on the path of success. Not only was this distracting from the ultimate task immediately at hand (playing my best golf), but also it was a wishful and hopeless pursuit because there is never *one* component that will always produce your best results.

Beyond the lackluster results of being others-focused, this mindset was incredibly exhausting. Every week held new ideas to try out, new components of the swing to incorporate, new strategies to consider. Rabbits were running everywhere, and I found myself constantly running down their trails.

In the midst of this endless pursuit, the one idea that saved me from myself was the concept of "systems."

DISCOVERING SYSTEMS

If Coach Jason was the initial voice for helping me see the need for systems and structures for success, then my swing coach as a professional, John Ray Leary, was the catalyst for finally understanding the importance of developing my own *personal* systems for success. Coach Jason planted the seeds for this personalized version during college, but Coach JRL solidified it in my mind and understanding.

Part of my struggle in chasing every rabbit trail was my pursuit of *ideals*. Ideals aren't bad, but reality is different. Understanding that I shouldn't expect to achieve the ideal, or even make it my goal to do so, took a long time for me to grasp. Let me explain what I mean.

Growing up I always played a draw (hitting shots that move from right to left in the air). This was my natural shot shape. As I began playing in college, I started wanting to hit more fades (moving the ball from left to right). This was extremely challenging for me since it was the opposite of what I had done my whole life, but I viewed it as a limiting factor for my success and fought to add it to my toolbox. This also led me to start including the shot during competitive rounds, even if it wasn't the wise shot to make—and it rarely was.

The bottom line is this: I always wanted what I didn't have. The grass was always greener in another player's game and ability. The magic elixir seemed to always reside in the skills just outside of my current skill set. This was the self-limiting belief that Coach JRL helped me discover. At the end of the day, the number on the scorecard is just that: a number. And numbers don't reveal the narrative behind how that number came to be. So *how* you get the ball in the hole isn't as important as simply *getting* the ball in the hole. It is one thing to conceptually agree and another to accurately apply it to daily practice and competition.

Halfway through my professional career, the practical application of this concept began to unfold. My heightened focus on others finally reached consciousness, and self-awareness entered the picture. After seeing this focus for the hindrance it was, I began the fight to change the mental habits around how I operate within competition and playing golf as a whole. I wanted to lean into my strengths in order to maximize my ability, just as both coaches had advised and instructed all along.

This led me down the path of self-discovery, so to speak, with the understanding that playing my best was really just that: *my* best. In order to play my best, I had to know what was best *for me*. And that meant that, at a certain point, I needed to look inward to find it, not outward.

CONCEPT

"You can achieve anything you want in life if you have the courage to dream it, the intelligence to make a realistic plan, and the will to see that plan through to the end."
—Sidney Friedman

WHAT MAKES A GOOD GOLFER?

Here is a question I was recently asked: What makes a good golfer?

The immediate thought that followed was, how do you attempt to answer a question like that?

As I considered an appropriate response, many possible answers floated to the surface: Patience is needed. Practice is required. Endurance is a component. Confidence must be present. Focus is necessary.

As with most words we use in day-to-day conversation, concepts can carry a nebulous meaning, easily understood but not so readily defined. In answering a question like "what makes a good golfer?" (or financial advisor, or artist, or engineer, nurse, employee, etc.), the answer will inevitably fall into one of two categories.

When examining the world's leading entrepreneurs and innovators, clear differences can be seen. Elon Musk and Steve Jobs would likely share many of the same traits and attributes, yet they undoubtedly have many differences, both in how and in what they produce. Looking specifically at golf, the same could be said about Tiger Woods and Phil Mickelson. Both are world-renowned players who will go down as two of the best golfers of their generation. So if we ask, "What makes Tiger and Phil good golfers?" we can highlight many shared characteristics that contribute to their success on the golf course, but there are equally as many differences in the ways they achieve that success.

The point is this: In any field, sport, craft, business, or trade, there are both *universal principles* and *individual principles* that lead to success.

WHAT'S MOST IMPORTANT?

So, since there are two options, which is most important?

At this point, I want to remind you of the journey we are on. It is the quest for mastery, in some form or fashion. On this path, we move from simplicity to complexity and then finally back to simplicity. The flow within this book follows a parallel process. In reaching this chapter, we are beginning the arduous process of moving toward that simplicity on the far side of complexity. This process involves further application of *discernment,* first discussed in chapter 4.

Everyone wants the silver bullet. We all want to know what *the* answer to *the* question is. If anything was that easy, then no one would ever want it. We long to accomplish lofty endeavors but are often unwilling to accept (or even acknowledge) the fact that those goals will lead us down a challenging, stretching, and soul-straining road. It isn't the path of least resistance but likely the path of most resistance. Simply stated, it takes *effort*, and lots of it.

Any question such as "what makes a good golfer?" or "what's most important?" carries with it this tension. The answer that's accompanied by a cop-out chuckle is yes (indicating it's a combination of the two options), which almost always means living in some sort of tension.

Before I offer an answer, I want to give a bit more description behind what the two categories represent.

Universal principles are the fundamentals commonly accepted as the requirements for success, things everyone should strive to emulate in some form or fashion. To be a good golfer, it is universally accepted that you must have a good short game (putting and chipping), carry an infallible confidence in your own ability, spend enough time practicing to ingrain muscle memory needed for consistent repetition (aka a *ton* of practice), gain experience for knowing how to handle competing with pressure, and on, and on. These are just a few snippets to show what universal principles contribute to a golfer's title of "good" (or "great").

Individual principles are the aspects tailored to your personality and your individual strengths/weaknesses. As much as Tiger and Phil have in common, the fact still stands that they are two drastically different people. Thus, what they do will inherently carry many differences, while still sharing the goal of maximizing their potential and producing the best golf possible.

Some people are more introverted, others more extroverted. Some people work better in isolation, while some prefer the group setting. Some people are thinkers and others are purely doers. Some people like mental (brain) work, and others like physical (body) work. Some people like working to live, whereas others live to work. Some people work best in conflict, and others in agreement.

So for me, or anyone else, to say that everyone *must* replicate every aspect of Michael Jordan's / Bill Gates's / Warren Buffet's / Beyonce's / fill-in-the-blank's principles, habits, routines, and experiences in order to produce the same measure of success they've accomplished is insanity. Because the reality is, no two people travel the same path. "Twinning" is not an ingredient for success. To be *your* best, you have to be *you*.

What am I saying? My point is this: *both* universal *and* individual principles are needed for success.

TIME TO DEFINE

Once we've been taught the universal principles needed for success, then we must press on toward discovering our individual system for success. But before I move to specifics, we need to first understand the concepts underlying both "systems" and "success."

First, what is a system? For our purposes, it is best defined as "a set of principles or procedures according to which something is done; an organized scheme or method." It is a series or group of habits, routines, or disciplines that lead to a desired result or product. The purpose of a system is to consistently maximize (beneficial) output. In theory, having a system that defines the best way to produce X, Y, or Z helps us follow proven methods for getting there. We need assistance and accountability to help us follow this path because of how easily we're distracted, misled, or deceived. When left to ourselves, chaos can creep into the scene unnoticed. Entropy *is* the default reality, and degradation is the natural progression if structures aren't formed and followed.

The more challenging term to define is "success."

What is success? From a textbook standpoint, success is defined as "the accomplishment of an aim or purpose." It's predictably basic—but that's the point. Success cannot be universally defined because it is inextricably tied to our individual values. Success looks drastically different from person to person. For myself, as a follower of Jesus Christ, success is defined as loving God above all, and loving others more than myself. It is a theological definition given to me by my faith. But for you it may look like something drastically different.

What's important to remember is that we need to *actually* define success. If we never specifically, intentionally, and individually define success, then we will adopt the culture's view of what it means, whether or not we personally agree. This ties back to our foundation. If we don't start with why—our purpose for what we are pursuing (which is synonymously attached to our definition of success)—then we are building a career (and our lives) on sandy ground, ripe for erosion and decay.

Knock, knock. Who's there? Entropy, the friend of those who don't care.

HOW DO WE GET THERE?

As with definitions, there's always a *process* involved—a "series of actions or steps taken in order to achieve a particular end." When we know the process, we will better understand how to end up at our desired destination.

When developing *your* personal system for success, there are two phases: (1) adoption, and (2) creation. While these are important phases, the precious pearl is really found in the space between—in the transition from the first stage to the second stage. But before that, let's talk about what these two phases entail.

1. *Adoption*

Early on, you must work to adopt the systems for success given to you from your coach, teacher, school system, job description/requirements, company protocols, boss's wishes, etc. The whole point of these relationships is to impart a system or structure for the task at hand so that, as you learn to do the given task/responsibility well, you can avoid the common pitfalls or mistakes you'd naturally fall into without instruction. The people in these positions have been given authority because they have the experience, knowledge, or skill you are working on developing. They can help you get there faster than you could by yourself.

This was the phase of my golf career when I entered into the world of collegiate competition. Coach Jason was the person who instilled in me the systems for success that he learned throughout his own career and experience, in order to help me perform my best in a shorter length of time than I could accomplish without his instruction.

Obviously, the most important trait in adoption is *teachability* (see chapter 4). You must be humbly submissive to instruction and guidance in order to *receive* it. And if you never *willingly* receive it, then you'll never benefit from it. In fact, when we aren't teachable, we end up producing both inner strife and outer turmoil from the constant clashing with the authorities that be, which does nothing to help us (or anyone else) get better.

Adoption is not a process that can be sped through. It is a period of patient acquisition when you comprehensively learn from the system given to you so that you're able to understand the benefit it brings, both intellectually and experientially.

Patience is the key to successfully adopting prescribed systems for success. Naturally, we think we know best, and when we instinctively disagree with what we're being taught, we begin at a place of cynical disbelief. This creates a rocky road, forcing us to fight our instinct in order to actually learn and benefit from what's being given to us—a fight that doesn't have to be fought. In contrast, responding with humble acceptance allows us to immediately get to the work of applying the given methods to know and experience their true worth.

2. *Creation*

Once you've spent the time, energy, and effort to fully adopt and integrate prescribed systems, then the next step forward is the creation of your own *personal* system. The creation phase will be most effective after you've spent an adequate amount of time in the adoption phase—a time in which, ideally, you've learned from multiple systems in several different environments.

This is the launching point for simplicity on the far side of complexity. It's when you begin to personally curate and craft your own system for success, ultimately accomplishing your goals more effectively and efficiently. Even if you're still in a position under a higher authority or structure, creating your own systems can still be helpful, but only if the system you create accomplishes the goals and desires of your superiors quicker and easier.

You may be thinking, *This seems too easy.* And you're right! There is a substantial gap between these two phases that isn't easily bridged. In that very expanse lies the real journey that must take place in order to understand how to develop your own system for success—the journey of knowing thyself.

THE SPACE IN-BETWEEN

> *"There are three things extremely hard: steel, a diamond, and to know one's self."*
> —Benjamin Franklin

In moving from adoption to creation, there is an ocean that must be traversed. It is the voyage of developing *self-awareness*: knowing yourself.

This is not a new concept, and it definitely isn't a concept I came up with. From the ancient world to the present age, being able to objectively see and introspectively know yourself is widely attributed as a key indicator for wisdom and success.

Greek philosophers held this idea near and dear. Socrates stated it most simply: "Know thyself." Aristotle, who followed under the tutelage of Plato (who was a student of Socrates), added to this by saying, "Knowing yourself is the beginning of all wisdom." In a parallel realm of history, Lao-Tzu (thought of as the founder of Taoism) said, "He who knows others is wise; he who know himself is enlightened."

Enlightenment is the state of having knowledge or understanding. Wisdom is simplistically seen as the proper application of knowledge. Self-awareness, then, can be seen as a shared precursor for cultivating wisdom and progressing toward enlightenment.

That's the big-picture view of self-awareness, but I want to talk about the small picture—the here and now of what self-awareness means.

Self-awareness is required as a prerequisite for the creation phase. Why? Because, in order to know the best systems to create, you *must* have a keen and heightened level of self-awareness. And "best" means best—finding the right solution to your own self-made problem of how you operate. This is a product of the human condition. We are created with unique and individual personalities, which means that we each have strengths and weaknesses that must be recognized and known. In order to know our unique self, we must develop an accurate self-awareness. This will then allow us to create, inform, and grow our instinct (intuition) into an accurate guide.

Intuition is a massively helpful muscle to train and develop. If self-awareness is the ocean we are traversing, then storms are inevitable. In order to find the land beyond our visible horizon, we must have a trusty compass to guide us through the waves and currents that seek to redirect our path. It is this gut-level instinct that helps us accurately navigate across the sea of self-awareness, en route to the creation of our unique system for success.

But it is important to note that intuition is not innate. Rather, it is a developed and refined skill that comes as a result of amassed experience. The deeper the knowledge and the greater the experience we have with a skill, or within a given field, then the stronger our gut instinct will be, and the greater trust we can place in its guidance.

THE STAGES OF SELF-AWARENESS

By now, you may be able to guess the path for developing self-awareness—simplicity, complexity, simplicity.

Early on in this process, you are simply trying to observe yourself more, becoming aware of how your subconscious works and how you come to the decisions you make or the actions you take. These observations should carry an increasing level of objectivity and regularity.

As your self-understanding grows, you will begin to have a clearer picture of what your individual strengths and weaknesses are. This can be both helpful and harmful. Sometimes the more we know, the more we become trapped inside our mind. This is when the pendulum of self-awareness swings toward the side of hyper-awareness—a state of self-consciousness that results in more inaction than action. When your existence primarily resides between your ears and not in everyday life, then you end up lost within the complexities of your mind and become a self-enclosed human who is of limited service to anyone outside of your own headspace.

This is an imbalance that needs correction. Imbalances are a part of life, which is why we must become skilled at recognizing and then correcting those areas that impair our homeostasis.

To keep out of the black hole that comes from introspective deep dives, you must train yourself to be *situationally aware*. This means that you are able to *curate* self-awareness—specifically choosing when to be self-conscious and when to be fully present and engaged with the world and people around you. This situational awareness is made possible by *discipline*.

Discipline is required to keep our minds in check. This means that when we feel prompted to self-examination but know it won't be helpful in the present moment, we force our minds to stay focused on what is happening externally. This does not mean that we fully avoid or become numb to all self-awareness practices, but rather that we intentionally schedule them for the times when they provide the most benefit to us and the least detriment to others. This is made possible by designating specific time-slots for *reflection*.

Much more to come on reflection.

APPLICATION

"There are no secrets to success. It is the result of preparation, hard work and learning from failure."
—Colin Powell

If I had read the concepts I just gave during college, I don't think much would have changed. Hearing or reading isn't the same as applying, and information is only as good as its use in daily living. The beauty of playing professional golf was that it *forced* me to apply these concepts. If I hadn't changed my focus from what others were doing to what I needed to do, then I would have continued producing lackluster results and wasting both time and money—both of which are limited resources.

The ideas I'm about to share are ways to help us develop our own personal systems for success. They are ideas that come directly from what I developed playing professional golf, and while I wish I could say otherwise, they were not developed intentionally. As with most insights, it was something I fell into it.

One of the most powerful concepts mentioned earlier is reflection. Reflection was a habit I developed in order to write blog posts for friends, family, and fans, keeping them updated on my results and career. I never thought about how important dedicating time to reflection was, or how it facilitated learning, development, and greater self-awareness. But slowly and surely, over the years this habit turned into one of the greatest growth factors in all of life. Beyond growth, it became the main stepping-stone to me writing this book.

I mention all of that to say that this is *important*. It is worthy of your consideration, and I know wholeheartedly how it can be a vital skill that will lead to your own growth and success.

DEVELOPING SELF-AWARENESS

Knowing how to get there is often as important as knowing where you're going. In creating a habit of self-awareness, there are some helpful road markers to use for guidance.

Here are the road markers to look for:

- *Prerequisite—*
  In order for self-awareness to be useful, you need to be in the complexity stage of maturity. This means that you have a good foundation built of knowledge/skill, you're able to learn effectively, you're teachable, and you have a basic understanding of

the overall journey and with your current place in it. Simply put, you have reached a threshold of proficiency that allows introspection to be useful in your life.

- *Starts (and ends) with reflection—*
  This is the nonnegotiable; it cannot be replaced. You must understand where you've come from, what you've been shaped by, and how you've developed into the person you currently portray. This is done almost entirely by reflection. As you develop this practice, it will provide you with a base level of objectivity that will facilitate an honest view of your own perspective.

- *Seek conflict—*
  There are many ways we deceive ourselves, and as a result of confirmation bias, we rarely see our self-deception until we are opposed or exposed. We need healthy conflict in our life to show us what should or shouldn't be important to us. This conflict can be found in conversations, books, ideas, beliefs, styles, entertainment, people, etc. When we surround ourselves with more and more versions of "ourself" (aka mini-me's), we continually narrow the scope of our worldview and stunt our self-awareness in the process. The end sum of this game is ignorance, not bliss.

- *Seek challenge—*
  The only way we can see our weaknesses or limitations is to expose them through challenge. We must stretch ourselves, pushing the boundaries of what we think is personally possible to help us understand our self-imposed limitations—both what's real and what's fabricated. If you begin to treat self-awareness as a muscle, then you start to see the need for adding that extra plate on the bar, because you won't get stronger unless you add more weight. Challenge yourself in order to greater understand yourself.

- *Seek outside perspective—*
  Blind spots are simply just that: blind. We can't see them by our own efforts; we need help. When driving, we use our mirrors to help us see, but the prevailing blindspot requires us to turn around and look over our shoulder to make sure we didn't miss a vehicle hidden from the mirror. Asking others for feedback

or constructive criticism is that look over our shoulder that we need to verify we're not missing something that might jeopardize our well-being. And in turn, we increase our objectivity and awareness of ourself.

- *Use tools—*
Nowadays, there are a plethora of self-tests that can classify and quantify our internal wirings. While these should not be treated as divine revelation, they can be very helpful for increasing our understanding of ourselves. These come in many shapes and sizes (personality tests, strengths finder, etc.), but most will have some level of benefit. At a certain point, there is a law of diminishing returns: when self-quantification creates more complexity and nuance than needed, there will be a reduction of usefulness found in confusion rather than clarity. Nonetheless, tools have their purpose and can be of use.

- *Learn from living—*
Learning comes from both *knowledge* and *experience*. In post-education life, these are best exemplified by two endeavors: (1) reading, and (2) traveling. Reading is the cheapest form of education. Books provide a perspective that enables us to see our own perspective in a new light. Through reading various types of books and authors, we gain greater self-awareness by interacting with the worldviews and ideas they present. On the other hand, traveling is the most heightened form of experiential education that lasts throughout our life. Traveling to a new environment reveals a new culture (or subset within our current culture) while simultaneously giving us a more accurate view of our own culture and it's unique nuances. Both reading and traveling can be powerful stimulants for self-awareness. It's the natural mentor of a life lived with intention.

- *Practice humility—*
Pride breeds ignorance, and ignorance is a direct assailant of self-awareness. A life filled with ignorance will be a life subjected to self-deception. If we aren't consciously directing our fight against pride, then we will naturally fall into its grasp. Humility must be nurtured, cultivated, and developed as a necessary part of our practice of self-awareness.

- *Value listening above talking—*
  Learning to be a good listener is an honorable life skill. Listening more than speaking is often the fruit of a humble spirit. It shows that we don't know it all and that we're seeking to learn before seeking to instruct, correct, or inform. It is a simple way to help us help ourself. In seeking to hear and understand the other person, we internally practice self-awareness by how we interpret what they say, while gaining a deeper understanding of our personal worldview filtration system.

It's worth mentioning the process for using self-awareness as a growth stimulant. It is a simple, four-step path: (1) observe, (2) evaluate, (3) correct, and (4) ingrain. Self-awareness in and of itself is a good thing, *but it is only as helpful as the change it produces.* **Observation** (step 1) is important, but, for it to provide personal benefit, you must also **evaluate** (step 2) whether what you see in yourself is helpful or hurtful, and then implement the **correction** (step 3) required to align who you really are with who you want to be. Finally, you must patiently commit to this correction for as long as needed to **ingrain** (step 4) this new form of self into reality.

THE KEY TO UNLEASHING SELF-AWARENESS

"Those who cannot remember the past are condemned to repeat it."
—George Santayana (Spanish-American philosopher)

History is a helpful picture of the value found in self-awareness.

Historical recurrence is a fond topic among the renowned minds of time present and time past, and for good reason. The devaluation of history seems to be one of the prevailing historical recurrences, witnessed time and time again. If we had a greater awareness of our ignorance regarding history, then we could work on reducing the negative recurrences and increasing the positive recurrences.

The simpler way to say it is this: *we must use the past to inform the present about what we want the future to be.* But if we never even look to the past, then we won't have an accurate guide for reaching future goals, all while living in a present ignorance.

Historical recurrence is a large-scale picture of what happens within each individual on the path toward self-awareness. This key that unlocks the door to self-awareness is held in one word: *reflection.*

Visual acuity is defined as: "sharpness of vision, measured by the ability to discern letters or numbers at a given distance according to a fixed standard." This is used as a rubric for determining our eyesight and whether we need some form of corrective lens to return clarity to our vision. Reflection is the contact lens to the eyes of life. It provides a clearer sight of prior situations and life experiences, largely due to the absence of distracting emotions found when we're "in the moment." This objectivity is the reason why we love the adage "hindsight is 20/20."

There are several secondary benefits to the practice of reflection.

First, it frees us up to be fully engaged and present in the moment to moment of everyday life. When we know there will be designated time later on to reflect and evaluate, we can remove the distraction of evaluating ourselves in the moment and can maximize our presentness with the people or tasks at hand.

Second, it forces us to learn in several different ways:

1. *Experiencing*—The way we learn from the experiences in life is by taking time to remember and remind ourselves of what happened and what it taught us.

2. *Vocalizing (written)*—In writing down what has happened and our thoughts on it, we are using a form of vocalization, communicating through writing what we learned, which strengthens the neural connections—aka your ability to remember and truly learn.

3. *Implanting*—Reflection is also an important time to implant the corrective ideas and thoughts needed to change, which increases the benefit from its practice. This is literally a form of preaching to yourself.

4. *Repeating*—The more you practice reflection, the more you start seeing the recurring themes. Repetition, in both observation and implantation, is a stimulant and solidifier for helping information stick.

5. *Compounding*—The more you reflect, the more you see repeated themes, the more you preach to yourself, the more your self-awareness grows, the more your life awareness grows, and the more it exponentially compounds into mental models and an informed, conscious view of the world.

6. *Clarifying*—Life is filled with endless noise. Distractions abound, and thus we must cut through the crap to see what's worth focusing on. Reflection enables us to live with clarification in mind.

Finally, reflection creates a scheduled time to sit with our thoughts. This can be scary. Many times, entertainment (TV shows, social media, magazines, etc.) is the escape method we use to *not* be left alone with our mind. Changing this pattern is difficult, especially since it's *counter-cultural*. Experiencing life with a pure and unfiltered presence is both terrifying and invigorating. But, as with most things in our increasingly full lives, if it isn't scheduled into our daily planner or calendar, then it likely won't happen.

Reflection is the answer.

WHAT STANDS IN OUR WAY

Forming the habit of reflection is not an easy task, and many things stand in the way of making time for the discipline of reflection. Here are some of the obstacles we face:

- *Don't see the immediate value*—The majority of people don't see the benefit or value in reserving time for reflection. If we don't see the benefit, then there's no reason to implement a new activity, especially one that isn't easy or entertaining. And beyond that, there isn't a ton of *immediate* benefit. Much of reflection's usefulness comes in the long-term cumulative effect.

- *Seems like a poor use of time*—Spending time looking backwards doesn't intuitively sound like a tool for helping us move forward. This is why we have to convince ourselves that it's worth the sacrifice of time first, and then allow the future benefit to accrue in due time—delaying immediate gratification for long-term reward.

- *Laziness*—Reflection, like any discipline, takes work. Our internal resident—laziness—will not be happy to see an additional task on the to-do list, *especially* since it's a task that is only seen by yourself, garnering no praise from others.

- *Competing distractions*—With so much information vying for our attention, discretion is of the utmost importance when choosing what to pay attention to. If we don't actively determine attentional worth, then the best attention grabbers will make the decision for us (social media anyone?). Saying no to distractions is what allows us to say yes to disciplines.

- *Unwanted discomfort*—As I mentioned already, reflection can be a scary endeavor. Most people shy away from discomfort, when in reality, discomfort is the needed stimulant for personal growth. In its absence, stagnation ensues. We need to embrace the idea of discomfort in order to bravely look at the monster within. But be warned: your arch-nemesis—discomfort—may soon become your best friend.

- *Acting in the minority*—We are inherently crowd followers. Going against the current and acting in opposition to the majority take intentional effort. The majority of people want nothing to do with reflection. In order to embrace the minority, we must understand that just because most people won't make reflection a personal discipline, that doesn't mean we shouldn't embrace it in our own lives. Dare to be different.

- *Thoughtless living*—Most of the cultural messaging we hear encourages us to listen to our feelings and emotions above all else. This produces a life of thoughtlessness, living by how we feel versus what we know. Reflection does involve a recognition of our emotions, but it requires thought*ful*ness in moving from feelings to a logical assessment of their effects—hence, self-awareness.

- *The scatterbrained struggle-bus*—This is a description of the mental state where most of us reside. In the context of modern society, the ability to focus is disappearing before our very eyes.

Attention spans are falling faster than sub-prime mortgages did in 2008. Early on, reflection will be a rocky road. It will be a fight, with daily battles being won and lost (usually beginning with more losses than victories). But reflection, with it's compounding nature (reference section above), will be a tool that enables a greater degree of focus as our mental discipline improves from the practice of examining the past.

Recognize what walls stand in your way and then, as Jocko Willink proudly commands, don't just climb *over* the walls; hit the obstacles with a sledgehammer and bust *through* them.

"Let your schedule govern your actions, not your level of motivation."
—James Clear

CREATING YOUR SYSTEM

We've finally made it to phase two: creation. Creating will always be an adventure. Some see it as pure bliss while others see it as a daunting endeavor. Whichever your view, this phase is characterized by many series of trial and error. The development of self-awareness does not replace the value of experience in learning what works best for your specific needs. At some point, we have to get our hands dirty and see which seeds bear fruit and which don't live up to the hype.

Here's what the process entails:

Throughout our journey in life, we've undoubtedly been exposed to a plethora of systems, ideas, and information. Once we've reached an adequate understanding of ourself, we must begin to *evaluate* the personal usefulness of the systems (or components within the systems). This entails pinpointing (*targeting*) the ideas or habits with the most potential for personal and specific application.

After targeting, we must knuckle down and do the work of *implementing* these new protocols into our *daily* life. This is where the fight begins. Commitment must always be fought for, and when we submit a new habit for incorporation, there will undoubtedly be kickback. We must not allow our feelings to interfere with the steadfast commitment of applying that's needed to solidify new habits. This is massively important because, for the new system's true merit to be seen, there must be a duration long enough to truly evaluate it. The cliche "time will tell", is true. For the true fruit to be known, there must be adequate time spent experiencing the *integration* of it in life so that we can be objective in our jurisdiction. Patience is vital.

When *examining* the worth of our new habit, we must use discernment in knowing what parts (or whole) to keep (what provided benefit) and what deserves to be discarded. This is another challenging task. Discarding the incorporated systems that didn't produce the anticipated level of benefit will feel like sacrificing a child, especially in the early stages of creation. After putting in the blood, sweat, and tears to incorporate the habit into your life, throwing it away seems like such a waste. But saying yes needs to be reserved only for the habits of highest personal value. The good news is that as you learn to incorporate more things in and out of your life, the easier it will become and the better you get at saying no.

This is the process.

Reflect - Evaluate - Target - Implement - Integrate - Examine - Repeat

The final part is to simply *repeat* it throughout our lives. Repetition is not a trivial part. This is not something we grow out of as we add digits to our age. It is something that's always needed for reaching our highest potential—*especially* with each stage of life (and really every year of life) being so different, morphing and changing and creating and challenging us in unique ways.

THINGS TO NOTE

Creation is a phase that doesn't carry strict guidelines. It is *fluid*—changing within the space that contains it, flowing freely down the path of least resistance. But there are some important things to remember about this phase.

Seasons Change

As mentioned earlier, your systems will change (or shift) as the seasons of your life change. The systems you create at 25 will likely lose much of their benefit at age 45 (and maybe even at age 27). This is not to say that there won't be systems that stand the test of time, lasting throughout your life, but it is to say that a majority of your systems won't. This is another useful motivator to be a life-long learner. May we strive to be learning and relearning new concepts, ideas, systems, and habits our entire life!

Experimentation Is Hard
Trying new things is never easy, mostly because it requires more effort than sticking to what we know. Building the habit of experimentation will help you choose the path of more resistance more often. But the difficulty doesn't change with age. In fact, it will likely grow more challenging the older you become. Never let the difficulty keep you from experiencing the fruit of creating your best systems.

Systems Are Not Valuable
Yes, this chapter was all about the importance of systems to create success, but the inherent value is not found in the system itself. The value is always found in the *result* the system produces. This is an important distinction. Sometimes you can begin to create systems merely to create systems. The point of any system is to produce a certain result, but when we start putting value on the system itself, we lose its effectiveness and become obsessed with systems instead of results. Always begin with the end in mind. Aim for results, not systems.

Goals Are Needed
Goals are the fertilizer for creating and sustaining systems. As with the changing seasons of life, goals are always shifting. Sometimes goals can be 5, 10, or 15 years down the road. But most of the time, goals are daily, weekly, or monthly. With specific goals come specific systems to help accomplish them efficiently and effectively. Recognize the inextricable link between your goals and your systems in order to discard the unneeded systems once the goal has been reached or shifted.

Systems Have Thresholds
Many of the systems that are implemented will have thresholds. These thresholds can be present on the front-end as well as the back-end. On the front-end, there is a threshold of effectiveness that must be passed in order to see the true merit of the habit you're fighting to ingrain. On the back-end, many systems will have a threshold that, once reached, results in the reduction of implementation needed to keep producing the desired result. Once you become a concert pianist, there is less skill prac-

tice needed to maintain a high level of mastery in your craft. Of course, to be elite in any endeavor, you must continually pour yourself into all components involved, but for singular goals, there is often a threshold of usefulness. This can be a helpful guide in knowing when to drop certain systems and when to hang on.

THE HABITS TO RULE THEM ALL

With the changing of seasons, habits will come and go. But there are certain systems and habits that stand the test of time. These are the pillars we can rest on to hold us steady in the midst of uncertainty and the unexpected nature of life. They are known as *cornerstone habits*.

Cornerstones (also called "foundation stones") were formerly used in masonry construction. These were the most important part of the foundation, because every other stone that was laid would be based on the one cornerstone. With the cornerstone in its proper place, the building was destined for success, but without it, the building would be set up for failure.

Cornerstone habits are the practices and routines that hold the rest of our life together. They create the anchor we need in times when the storms are upon us. These habits are the nonnegotiable elements within our entire system for success, the parts of our lives that impact the rest of our lives in the most influential and pervasive way.

Inevitably, these cornerstone habits *must* be tied to your why. They must be rooted and grounded in your purpose in life, which is what holds them fast and keeps them close. This connection is fuel, providing motivation to always foster and maintain their presence. It's what creates their true value.

While everyone's cornerstone habits will look different, here are what mine entail:

- Starting and ending each day by reading God's Word—the Bible.
- Getting an adequate amount of sleep every night (and if not, catching up within a few days time)
- Daily and weekly discipline of physical exercise

- Eating food, consciously and intentionally, that is best for my body
- Making time for reflection, daily
- Consistently incorporating "priming" before any activity/endeavor

These are the tools that keep my life in alignment to my core purpose and values, and they facilitate everything else to be done to my very best under that alignment.

If you haven't yet set the cornerstone, start there. The rest of the building will follow.

Phase Three: Simplicity

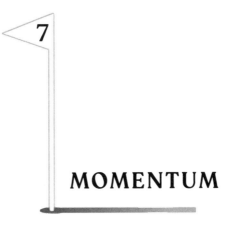

MOMENTUM

"Momentum solves 80% of your problems."
—JOHN C. MAXWELL

"Golf is the closest game to the game we call life. You get bad breaks from good shots; you get good breaks from bad shots—But you have to play the ball where it lies."
—BOBBY JONES

"Change and consistency are the two balancing weights on the seesaw of human experience, and God has given humanity the means to enjoy both of them by patterning the world with rhythm."
—DAVID GIBSON

"Resistance is proportionate to the size and speed of the change, not to whether the change is a favorable or unfavorable one."
—GEORGE LEONARD

MY STORY

Snowboarding is one of my true loves. It literally breathes life into me. Standing atop a towering mountain, surveying the beauty and wonder of the land unfolded before me, all covered in a serene and magical layer of white—words can't describe it. Even as I'm writing this, my mind is filled with images and memories of awe and wonder.

For true love to be love, it must be sacrificial. As with most things we love, I have definitely made sacrifices to preserve my relationship with snowboarding. Three broken wrists, many bruises and tweaks, and a rib injury later—the love has not only endured, but has also grown!

Yet, with reflecting upon this part of my life, there is one incident worth mentioning.

THE FALL

So there I was, in Crested Butte, Colorado. It was a briskly cold day with blue-bird skies and the sun shining brightly. I was on a church ski trip with my family and friends, and I couldn't have been happier. These were the days I lived for, all year long, and I was going to make the most of them. The harder I went, the better. As you might guess, it was not a sustainable mindset.

Since my family had gone on a trip with my grandparents to Crested Butte a month prior, I was familiar with the lay of the land and was ready to show off to all my buddies with the "local knowledge" I had.

One of the areas I wanted to show them was the park. The park is the place on the mountain where all the jumps are built and where all the rails and other features are placed. Being the self-proclaimed expert of the group, I triumphantly led them to the biggest park so that I could show them my prowess and guide them down their own journey of sending it off the jumps.

During the earlier trip with my family, there was an abundance of snow and several days of fresh powder. This makes the riding conditions much slower and more forgiving. On the church trip, there was little to no fresh snow, leaving us with hardpack and much faster conditions. Of course, being thirteen, this only registered in part of my brain.

Back to the park…

There we were, standing at the entrance to the park, all (secretly) looking sheepishly at the looming kickers (term for snowboard jumps) and features scattered below. Being the "local," I told everyone

I would show them the ropes. The funny thing about pride and testosterone is, they don't lead to a level head or clear thinking. As I made my way through the park, hitting the few jumps I felt comfortable with, I thought about how fast it felt that day. Yet, this realization didn't lead to action. I knew I had a bit too much speed heading into the third jump, but I decided I had to send it anyway, since all my friends were there watching.

The third jump was a stand-alone, step-up jump built on the side (you take off from a lower position than where you land). I figured that having too much speed wouldn't be an issue on a step-up jump like that. The caveat was, since it was a side jump, the landing was much shorter, flattening out within 10 to 15 feet after the ideal landing spot (whereas, most jumps' landings are very long to accommodate varying speeds). As I took off from the lip, I knew it would be an interesting few seconds ahead. While floating over the landing area, a small dose of anxiety and worry started to grow from my gut and move toward my brain.

As anyone familiar with extreme sports knows, landing in "the flats" often spells some sort of negative consequence. Bracing for impact, I tried to absorb what would inevitably be a *rough* landing. Since I had very little tangible experience in salvaging jumps gone bad, I didn't know exactly how to do that. As I landed on the flat hard-pack snow, the momentum of my speed, combined with the abrasive landing, bucked me forward, pitching me head first toward the ground in front of me. As I careened into the icy snow below, my arms came flying in hot pursuit. The landing sequence looked like this (in order of impact): board, bounce, body/arms (almost simultaneously, it was that fast), board, ego.

I knew the result of this whiplash immediately. There was absolutely no doubt in my mind: my right wrist had just fractured.

Momentum can be deadly.

THE TIME AFTER

But the story doesn't end there. I was a freshman in high school at the time, and that meant the high school golf season was fast approaching. Breaking my wrist in early February left enough recovery time to give me hope that I would be able to return for at least half of the season. Surgery, pins (and pain), casts, brace, recovery, rehab, and impatience marked the next few months.

My golf coach at the time, Charlie Pierce, was not pleased to find out about my wrist. Since I was a probable starter for the varsity team, recovering in time for the season was my number-one priority. But the road ahead was not for the fainthearted.

Once I finally got my cast off, my right wrist was barely recognizable. Size, mobility, color, smell—all had changed, and not for the better. In the game of golf, your wrists are one of the crucial points upon which the swing hinges. Combine that with a stiflingly cold Kansas in early spring (that makes all your bones feel every impact to the fourth degree), and with it being my first year playing on the high school team—what I got was a deck stacked entirely against me.

Playing against a stacked deck is *not* fun, but that is exactly where I found myself. At thirteen, I wasn't conscious of all that was going on—both in my mind and in the task before me; but looking back now, I can see how hard of a fight I was up against.

I had dug myself a deep, muddy hole that I was now tasked to climb out of. If my freshman year of golf was going to happen, I would have to claw myself out of the self-dug pit and then keep clawing my way up the slope ahead if I was ever to reach the level I aspired to. This battle was self-made, but the point shouldn't be whether a battle is self-made or not, because rarely will we consider a battle self-made, even if it is. A battle is still a battle, no matter who made it.

In these types of battles, there's a specific outcome we should be fighting to achieve. But it isn't what you might expect.

Instead of looking to defeat our enemy, we need to force our enemy to submit and then turn that enemy into our friend and our ally. We know how powerful this enemy is, and that's why we don't want to simply annihilate it; we want to convert it to our team and have it help us be the best that we can be.

This strange but powerful enemy is none other than *momentum*, and this chapter is all about how to start using it for good.

CONCEPT

Before we get to the smaller picture of understanding momentum in our lives, I want to first zoom out to see a global picture.

THE WORLD WE LIVE IN

In the modern world, it's hard to imagine the earth being flat.

Most assume the origin of a spherical earth began with Columbus, but theories on this reality began much earlier in the Greek world, originating with Aristotle and the likes in fourth-century BC. One of the well-known pioneers in this work was Eratosthenes, a Greek astronomer in third-century BC, who computed Earth's circumference from parallel measurements of the shadows cast by tall objects. Eratosthenes was followed by Ptolemy in second-century AD, who wrote *A Guide to Geography*, describing a spherical earth.

When something is flat, it is considered level. In geographical terms (apart from western Kansas), the majority of the United States would *not* be described in this way. In physical terms, referring to an object as flat often means some form of decreased utility—such as a flat tire or ball. Flat can also be descriptive of taste/texture. When a soda is considered flat, it is known to be bland in both taste and texture from the lack of carbonation. In terms of life versus death, "flatlining" is the medical term that pronounces a heart that's no longer beating and a body that's now without life.

With a general term such as "flat" come a multiplicity of meanings and synonyms. Some examples include the following: level, still, low, dull, monotonous, down, dejected, sluggish, inactive, unchanging, invariable, definite, plain, prone, unconditionally, and on and on. The point of understanding the word "flat" is to show how antonymous it is to life. From the physical realities of the world we live in to the physical functions of the bodies we inhabit, nothing is sustainably or unintentionally *flat*. When we realize *and* accept this fact, we begin to see that much of what we do is done with the goal of homeostasis ("the tendency toward a relatively stable equilibrium between interdependent elements, especially as maintained by physiological processes").

The world we live in is inherently capricious. Flatness is desired but rarely found. So where does that leave us?

THE BEAUTY OF LIFE

Images have varying degrees of flatness. There are one-, two-, three-, four-, five-, and six-dimensional objects (search "tesseract," "penteract," and "hexeract"). Out of these dimensions, the only two considered flat would be one- and two-dimensional images.

Imagine for a minute what it would be like to live in a one- or two-dimensional world…

…boring, dull, lifeless, limited—not a place I would want to live.

Why?

It would be a world without *life* (or, as Genesis 1 states, a world "formless and void"). A flat world is one that could be described as life-*less*.

The purpose of this argument is to show that the beauty in life is found in its variance. What it means to live is this: to experience, at different times and in different ways, both the mountain top and the valley low—feeling unparalleled exhilaration as well as life-crushing despair. This is what it means to be alive.

From geography to emotions to interpersonal relations, to physiological functions to creation to degradation and to renovation—these are the beautiful parts of what we all know as life. Without the bitterness of our darkest hours, the exuberance of our highest joys wouldn't carry the same awe and ecstasy.

Along with valuing the beauty of variance in life, we must also understand the component of sustainability. Life is best lived somewhere in the middle of the polar extremes. If we spend too much time in the darkness of the valley or too much time living on the mountain-top high, our life will break down and disappear before we know what hit us. In Steven Kotler's book, *The Rise of Superman*, he has an entire chapter dedicated to the "Dark Side of Flow." The point is that, if all we do is chase one side of momentum, without the needed balancing adjustments, then we will end up devaluing our life by taking risks we should never take, or ending life before it should be over. Why do you think so many extreme athletes die making this very mistake: going beyond their limits? And on the opposite end of the spectrum, we see the rise in suicide rates with those who are depressed, not wanting to forever remain in despair.

So while we are in a constant state of flux—moving toward a high, toward a low, or somewhere in between—we are always (or at least, *should always be*) working toward a place of balance. We simply can't achieve a life of seamless balance, nor should we! But we can use an awareness and understanding of our current place in the flow of life to help us adjust and start moving toward where we need to be. This results not only in a more sustainable life but also in a fuller and more effective life.

Steven Kotler said it well in that "[as] children we are taught *not* to play with fire, not *how* to play with fire" (*Rise of Superman*, p. 164). Being taught to avoid fire doesn't eliminate the reality of it in our life and the importance of fire to sustain life. Fire can be both a preserver of life and a destroyer of life.

This is precisely why an understanding of momentum is crucial. Momentum *cannot* be avoided. It's presence is inescapable. So instead of running into a safety net to try to eliminate as much variance as possible, we need to embrace momentum as our friend and lean into what it can bring.

WHERE ARE WE GOING?

In understanding what momentum is, we must now understand where we are going and then finally figure out how we can get there.

So, where are we going?

Here are four foundational elements we must recognize in order to use momentum successfully:

Foundation #1

The first step we must take is to *acknowledge* and *recognize* the place of momentum in our life. This means we accept and affirm it. The result is that we can no longer live in ignorance. More to come on ignorance, but let's first see some of the areas where momentum is present in day-to-day life:

- *Physiological*—There are times in the day when, due to hormones, digestion, energy expenditure/transfer, etc., we will be more prone to experience the feeling of highs or lows. This also includes energy levels related to both our circadian rhythms (day and night cycles of the body shifting from wakefulness to sleep and back again—occurs once daily) and our ultradian rhythms (which occur throughout the day, typically in 90 to 120-minute intervals, producing the resulting fluctuations in energy levels and biological functions).

- *Emotional*—All emotions are highly impacted by the experiences we encounter on a daily, moment-to-moment basis—from receiving bad/good news, to seeing something we agree/disagree with, to having something unexpected happen, and on and on it goes. Each day carries with it its own emotional roller-coaster ride.

- *Mental/physical capacities*—Some days we're on, and some days we are just off. Whatever your job is or whatever work you do, this is known and experienced by all. The key to success in golf is to play with what you've got. Specifically, this means to play in a manner that aligns with how on or off you are that day and then choosing your shots, strategy, and mindset accordingly.

- *Development*—This can apply to both personal development and business development. A good illustration of this is a child progressing through the various stages of infancy. It takes many weeks/months of crawling and testing out what it means to stand before she is finally able to stand on her own. After she reaches this milestone, her development begins to take off. Momentum is on her side and there is nothing she can't accomplish! The same is true with our own personal development. Malcom Gladwell refers to this point in time as the "tipping point"—when the ball reaches the crest of the hill and begins to use momentum from gravity to gain more and more speed as it races down the hill.

Foundation #2

Next, we must see momentum with *objectivity* and *gratitude*. Objectivity helps us avoid the desire to impose self-judgment on the cycles (good or bad) and, in turn, helps us adapt and improvise more fluidly to the ebbs and flows of life. Gratitude helps us gain the ability to use momentum as an asset instead of a liability, seeing it as the blessing it is.

Don't believe me? Here is a short list of what momentum gives us:

- *Perspective*—We wouldn't know the good without the bad, the joy without the sorrow. We need both to understand either.

- *Assistance*—Momentum gives us a speed boost towards our goal once we are able to get the ball moving down the hill. Who doesn't love a good turbo-boost?

- *Training*—As with the assistance momentum provides, it equally gives resistance. Resistance is needed to make us stronger, and momentum will sometimes work as our personal trainer.

- *Clarification*—Much of life can be distracting, but when we reach a valley or a mountaintop, what we experience clarifies reality, especially in the muddled space in between.

- *Unification*—Since momentum is felt by all, it can be an aspect of life that brings us together. We need others to help us in the highs and the lows just as much as we need to help others in those times. Momentum can be a powerful tool to unite.

- *Persistence*—Discipline is not an attribute given to us by birth; it is given through the experiences (highs and lows) of life. Persistence comes from climbing up and down enough mountains to attain the fruit of discipline.

- *Variance*—As already stated, a flat life is a life without *life*. Variance brings beauty, novelty, personality, difference, and similarity.

- *Hope*—Without the presence of variance in life—an earth in constant motion—there would be no hope. Hope is the anticipation or expectation of a desired future outcome. If all outcomes are the same then there's no need for hope. And a life without hope is a life not worth living.

Foundation #3

Now we must increase our *personal awareness* of momentum's presence in our life as well as our *situational awareness* of the day-to-day shifts as they take place. Without increased awareness and recognition, momentum will produce a *reactive* life instead of a *proactive* life.

Let's look a little further at the difference between reactive and proactive living:

- *Reactive*—This is the life lived in subservience to the will and wishes of the circumstance. A reactive life is one that responds in accordance to what took place, giving all control and authority to the situation and not the person.

- *Proactive*—This is the life lived under the conscious directing of your self. Instead of the circumstance being your master, you take control of your thoughts, emotions, and actions, regardless of the situation's influence.

Stephen Covey did a great job expounding this point in his book *The Seven Habits of Highly Effective People*. Writing about Victor Frankl's discovery, he says, "[A] fundamental principle about the nature of man is: *between stimulus and response, man has the freedom to choose*" (p. 70).

In comparing the state of being proactive to the state of being reactive, Covey writes, "[Proactivity] means more than merely taking initiative. It means that as human beings we are responsible for our own lives. Highly proactive people recognize that responsibility. They do not blame circumstances, conditions, or conditioning for their behavior. Their behavior is a product of their own conscious choice, based on values, rather than a product of their conditions, based on feeling." Comparatively, "reactive people are often affected by their physical environment ... and their social environment" (p. 71).

He goes on to say, "[R]eactive people are driven by feelings, by circumstances, by conditions, by their environment. Proactive people are driven by values—carefully thought about, selected and internalized values" (p. 72).

The simple summation of Covey's point is this: *it's a choice.*

Foundation #4

Finally, once we become aware of momentum and make the choice to replace reactive living with proactivity, we must then begin to use momentum as a *guide, tool,* and *teammate.* This will help us grow, adjust, learn, and accelerate beyond our perceived capacity, a capacity that didn't factor in momentum as an asset.

The bottom line is that momentum is impossible to avoid. It is part of the cyclical nature of life. Since you can't avoid it, you might as well start using it to your advantage. Because if you don't, know and trust that others will, and you'll be left breathing in their dust.

THE GUISE OF IGNORANCE

Ignorance is both prevalent and pervasive. So much so, many books can be (and have been) written on this reality. In the context of this chapter, there are two main subsets of ignorance: (1) intentional, and (2) unintentional. (Spoiler alert! Now that you're reading this chapter, you can no longer claim the latter.)

Unintentional ignorance is a result of simply not knowing any better. You don't know what you don't know, and there are periods of life when we can't help but not know. For example, no one gets angry at a child for crossing the street without looking; they get angry at the parent for not looking out for the child. Why? Because the child is unintentionally ignorant of traffic laws and procedures.

Intentional ignorance could be the title of any action that precedes the statement "you should know better than that." It's the intentional ignoring of what we know to be true. It's acting in accordance to what we *want* to do instead of what we *know* we *should* do.

Regarding momentum, it's vital that we're not ignorant of its influence. But as with most things, until someone helps us see the power and effect of the invisible forces at play, we can't begin to help ourselves.

They say that ignorance is bliss. I would argue the opposite. The life this phrase engenders can be understood as carefree living. But carefree living produces a life susceptible of being carried away by the cyclical momentum within life. Being directed by the world is the fruit of carefree living. Living with intention and ownership is the result of a life based on your why—your core purpose. Would you rather have control of the steering wheel or sit back and let life sweep you out to sea?

THE CYCLES: BIG PICTURE

In examining life's cyclical nature and how momentum factors into everyday performance and decisions, there are two helpful illustrations to keep in mind while walking through the cycles' descriptions.

The first is that of a mountain climber. Climbing a mountain is a very literal form of the ups and downs in life. It brings with it many hardships, exhilarations, dangers, adventures, struggles, and spurts of momentum, both helping and hurting your success along the way.

The second illustration to keep in mind is that of a roller coaster. As with mountaineering, riding a roller coaster has many ups and downs, twists and turns, which is what brings the thrill of the experience. However, when compared to mountain climbing, a roller-coaster ride is much shorter in duration and we have much less control while on the ride than we do during the climb. Each illustration rings true in different scenarios and situations we face, but both can provide useful pictures for us to learn from in understanding life's cycles.

While there are many different ways to define and describe the cycles present in life, here are the six cycles we will examine in this chapter:

1. Base/Neutral: beginning the journey
2. The Climb: growth or expansion edition
3. Peak/Mountaintop Experience
4. The Descent
5. The Valley Low
6. The Climb: fighting to resurface edition

It's easy to see the parallel in riding a roller coaster and climbing a mountain—always a series of ups and downs. The cycle of life ebbs and flows from childhood to old age. Once we start to understand this process, we begin to grow in awareness of its presence in our lives, and then, finally, we are able to consciously and proactively harness momentum to be used as an assistance rather than as a hindrance.

APPLICATION

The case I made in the beginning of this chapter was for the beauty of fluctuations. If we can see the good in momentum, then it will unlock our ability to *use* momentum to our advantage. Ultimately, whether it is to your advantage or not really isn't the point. The goal is to flourish in every season and phase of life—through the valleys and the peaks.

If you're like me, you may be thinking, *But why?* Or, *What is he even talking about?*

Before further explaining the six cycles, let's look at the origins of this mental framework that now guides my decisions and actions in life.

MOMENTUM IN GOLF

A major reason why golf is a sport parallel to life is because it's flat-out *hard*. In golf (and in life) there are no shortcuts. It is an exposing game, testing your mind, body, *and* character. While all the concepts in this book ultimately stem from what golf has taught me, the idea of momentum was uniquely highlighted in the game itself (as with most other sports).

One of the biggest challenges I faced as a professional golfer was momentum. Early on in my career, when I was looking to others for direction (or to copy their recipe for success), I could never seem to get momentum on my side, partly because I wasn't focused on it or even aware of it. On a macro scale, this was fueled by always looking to the next person to unveil the secret to success, but it was equally (and more dangerously) present on a micro scale within each round of golf I played.

Some of the smallest examples of killing momentum are known and hated by all who play the game. One example is found in missing a short putt (inside three feet) that should never be missed, followed by hitting your next tee shot out of bounds. Or allowing the danger of water ahead turn your focus from what you should be doing to what you *don't* want to do—thereby inevitably leading your ball to the pond's floor. These are a few of the classic examples of allowing negative momentum to help you underperform—a double negative that does *not* become a positive.

Looking at the bigger picture, most of my early years as a professional golfer revealed the fruit of poor momentum usage. One of the prevalent themes I see now was the intra-round flow. Typically, I would get off to a good start and be in good position midway through the round. But like clockwork, there would be some shot or some hole that would threaten to derail my round. More specifically (and importantly), what it really sought to derail was my *momentum*. The problem with not recognizing momentum is that you always succumb to its desires. Over time, I developed the wrong habit of allowing a bad shot to fester into a bad hole, which led to several bad holes, which was all that is needed to post a bad score, and none of those outcomes can be afforded as a professional.

This was the deadly cycle of momentum I found myself trapped in.

FROM GOLF TO LIFE

> *"While a good leader sustains momentum, a great leader increases it."*
> —John C. Maxwell

Looking back now, it is so easy to see it for what it is. It is *much* harder to recognize momentum in the moment-to-moment of our mundane daily lives. Having learned, firsthand, the negative consequences of failing to recognize momentum, I now know the importance of capitalizing on momentum and seeking the guidance it can provide.

Instead of going as hard as possible every time I step foot in the gym, I now listen to what my body is telling me it needs. When I've gotten a poor night of sleep (or several), I'm going to adjust my physical exertion in order to avoid the heightened risk of injury or of digging myself into a deeper hole than needed. This is momentum recognition.

When I am writing things (like this book), I now become aware of the times when I am in the zone, when the words and concepts are flowing fluidly and seamlessly. During times like this, I choose to prioritize my writing above all else and ride the wave of creative impulse as long as possible. This can last for several hours or as long as several days, or maybe even a week. Momentum recognition.

There are times when I know I need to be alone, and equally there are times when I need to be with others. After I get done working a long shift as a barista, interacting with many customers for hours on end (as with any customer-service industry), there's a good chance I need to prioritize time alone so that I can recharge my relational capacity to enable selfless love towards others. Momentum recognition.

Even beyond recognition and adjustment, momentum is a preparing force as well. When we miss several weeks of working out, the week we decide to return is always the worst. Knowing that I am going to feel awful both during the workouts and afterward, helps me mentally prepare my mind to endure. I have dug myself into a hole by not prioritizing the gym, so now I must gird up my loins and buckle down to do the work needed to get back on my feet with exercise. Momentum preparation.

THE CYCLES OF LIFE: DEFINITION AND KEYS

Now that you have a clearer picture of what I am talking about with momentum, let's take a further look at the six cycles that help illustrate different phases of momentum and how we should operate as a result.

1. Base/Neutral

Defined

This is the place in life when you are level. You are as balanced as you can be, neither progressing nor digressing (in the opinion of your self-assessment, which we know from the concept of entropy: if we're not progressing, then we are slowly digressing). This is where the majority of people strive to remain their entire lives, because, as we've repeatedly seen, the average performer's mindset is that security equals success (see chapter 2).

Typically, this is where people begin their journey of understanding and start seeking to team up with momentum. Once you begin the journey, rarely (if ever) will you return to a purely neutral state. The more you look, the more you'll find that you're always moving in one direction or the other. After you start to see momentum in your life, neutrality will only come when you ignore momentum, and ignorance is now something you can no longer claim.

Keys

- *Be grateful!*—Each and every part of the process is a blessing in its own way.

- *Begin moving towards something*—This can be a goal, target, idea, place, position, etc.

- *Challenge yourself* (aka become uncomfortable)—If you don't push yourself to start climbing upwards, then you'll begin by falling downward.

- *Understand that there's no going back*—Know that this is a lifestyle change; either you're moving or you're stagnant.

- While you may return to this stage for short periods of time, it should never be a prolonged state you remain in.

2. The Climb: growth/expansion edition

Defined

This is the upward progress of pushing toward something, the stage that is ushered in upon leaving neutrality. Climbing obviously takes work, and in this cycle you are putting in the effort to pursue the goal(s) set before you. As you progress in your climb, you are able to see both how far you've come and how much closer you are to reaching the peak. This dual reality stimulates and motivates you during the climb and helps you reach even higher heights.

When you think about climbing a mountain, the efforts expended to climb up, while still effortful, aren't associated with the negative aspects of work because of the joy that awaits upon reaching your destination. This is when the work is easy, fluid, and natural—carrying with it an intrinsically rewarding nature.

Keys

- *Be grateful*—This is one of the easier stages to experience gratitude, yet it is nonetheless important.

- *Use reflection as a stimulant*—Take time to look on the progress you've made to encourage and fuel more growth forward and upward.

- *Enjoy the work*—Lean into the rewarding joy found in challenging and fulfilling work.

- *Remain steadfast*—Be adamant and unwavering in carrying out your systems and completing the work before you.

- *Keep the end goal in sight*—Don't let your foot off the gas, and never lose the momentum you've generated thus far.

- *Cherish the anticipation*—Because that's where most of the pleasure in the pursuit is found.

3. Peak/Mountaintop Experience

<u>Defined</u>

As you take those final few steps, cresting the ultimate slope, you're met with the long-awaited panoramic landscape that is as vast as it is breathless. This is the moment when you've finally reached the summit of your climb. But, as is often the case in mountaineering, most summits are not the ultimate peak. Many times, reaching the summit is merely a pause before continuing up the mountain to an even higher summit ahead. There are varying levels of peaks that we will summit throughout our lives, but each experience should be cherished and remembered.

In life, this looks like accomplishing the goal you set out to achieve. Some goals are daily or weekly, and others are long-term endeavors that take years to reach. Regardless of the height of the peak, this is the culmination and climax of the reward you've been chasing.

<u>Keys</u>

- *Be grateful*—Yes, gratitude is needed in *every* stage.

- *Pause*—Take the time needed to properly appreciate where you have come and where you are now. This is harder than you'd imagine, partly because of the distracting nature of where you are in that moment.

- *Ingrain*—Capture the moment in its entirety: the image, feeling, sensations, etc. This is used for future times when that reminder is needed for further motivation.

- *Recognize its tenure*—It is important to realize the momentary nature of these experiences. This is one of the shorter cycles in life, and for obvious reasons. If we live in a never-ending high, the high loses its high.

- *Tarry but don't delay*—Strive to strike the balance between remaining in the moment for an adequate length of time to be present and to fully capture the moment, but don't delay departure beyond what is healthy for your journey ahead.

4. The Descent

Defined

This is a cycle where the components often vary. Anytime you are on a descent, it can be done in one of two ways: (1) carefully and cautiously working your way down, or (2) allowing gravity to take control and free-falling down the pitch. Initial judgment would say that option A is the best way down, but that's not always the case.

This is a good time to remember the roller-coaster illustration. On a roller coaster, the moment you reach the peak is when you finally let loose and begin the exhilaration of the ride. In life, we can use the momentum garnered from the descent in order to gain speed to propel us toward an even higher peak ahead. Once the ball gets rolling, it's much easier to keep it rolling. But, as a mountaineer, the descent can be a treacherous part of the journey. Coming off the mountaintop, you have less energy and less future incentive to look forward to, which leads to both heightened risk and reduced focus.

The descent is complex. It can be both dangerous and exhilarating. It's up to you to know which type of descent you're on and then to proceed accordingly.

Keys

- *Be grateful*—Enjoy the ride.
- *Know that there are always two ways to get down*: controlled, or uncontrolled.
- *Know which situations call for which response*: whether you are a mountaineer or a roller-coaster rider.
- *Respond accordingly*—If in a mountaineering situation, operate with controlled caution; if on a roller coaster, release control to momentum and let it carry you further with its force.

- *Understand what lies ahead*—Be prepared for the emotional low that usually follows any high. With proper preparation, we can handle the emotions and proactively use them instead of being reactively led by them.

- *Realize what's at stake*—This is arguably the most important stage. It can either be the most detrimental or the most beneficial to your overall journey.

5. The Valley Low

Defined

This is the cycle that's neither fun to talk about nor read, and it definitely is not the place anyone desires to be. Yet, it is as inescapable as it is dreaded. It is a place where everything lies in the darkness of the shadow, where the depths of despair loom. It is the time when you are drowning underwater and fighting for air, when the weight of the world (and of your own emotions) seems to be crushing you underneath.

Many times in life, things don't go our way, and it would be easy to argue that this is true more times than not. But much of the power of darkness is found in its unexpected nature. Life is never portrayed as an eternal struggle; it always promises more than it gives. The lows in life become most deadly when they are least expected. If we are prepared for the inevitable lows that accompany life as a human being, then we can weather the storm and come out stronger on the other side.

Keys

- *Be grateful*—In this cycle, all prior gratitude training will be tested by the fire. If you can't be grateful in the times of blessing, then it will be impossible to be grateful in the times of wanting.

- *Understand its universality*—The valleys are a natural part of life and the cycles it contains. Knowing this will help you see that you are not alone in this struggle.

- *Stop listening to emotions*—Especially in the lows, your emotions cannot be trusted as a guide. Strive to silence their voice so that you aren't led further astray.

- *Trust what you know*—During this cycle, faith should be put in what you know instead of what you feel. In the valley, your feelings will do more harm than good.

- *Reduce complexities*—Minimize the moving parts in your life to keep the chaos from even greater detriment or impact.

- *Realign or recommit*—Either find a new goal to align with or reestablish a prior goal to help tow you out of your current rut.

- *Learn*—The lows can be helpful and needed tutors to teach us how to further refine the other cycles in life. These are the lessons that provide the richest materials, no matter how unwanted they may be.

- *See the blessing*—When the going gets tough, the tough get going. We must understand that the low provides the opportunity to build character—work that's best done when everything else is stripped away.

- *Prepare for resurfacing*—Use the valley to strengthen resolve, motivation, and commitment for when you finally get above water.

- *Remember*—Store these experiences in your memory banks for future use. They will provide clarification on perspectives, help with empathy, deepen awareness, solidify core values, reveal unneeded/unwanted distractions, and refine who you are.

- *Sit with it*—Become comfortable with discomfort. Don't just see the value in it; work on becoming friends with it.

6. The Climb: fighting to resurface edition

Defined

This final cycle is when the rubber meets the road, when it's finally time to nut up or shut up. Get your Jocko Willink on and *man up!* This is truly the *fight* to get back above water. It is a day-by-day, moment-by-moment, clawing yourself up out of the ground—the time when you right the ship and get back on track, moving up and out toward your goals. Instead of external motivation being the main factor, it is internal motivation that will carry the load during this cycle. Guts, determination, discipline, and willpower are required.

Along with the difficulty of this cycle comes the necessity of it. This phase is required in life; we simply don't have a choice. The choice that we *do* have is how long we remain in it. The harder (and better) we fight, the faster we will win the battle and move past this part of the climb and back into one of the other cycles.

Keys

- *Be grateful*—This is not just a "pud" answer. This is a vital part of each cycle. We must develop gratitude for wherever we are in the roller coaster of life. If we don't appreciate what our present cycle provides, then we will never be able to use it proactively to our advantage. Each phase provides different advantages and disadvantages, teaching us a wide array of lessons.

- *Enjoy the fight* (which is a fight in and of itself!)—You can either fight out of duty and begrudgery or out of excitement and enjoyment of the opportunity it provides.

- *Adopt the farmer's mentality*—See the fight as fertile soil for planting the seeds of discipline. Nothing helps grow and solidify healthy habits and disciplines like a fight you don't have the choice in taking.

- *Become a better fighter*—Work on climbing better than the last time. Each return to this cycle provides an opportunity to improve on the last occasion.

- *Strive for perspective*—See the process as baby steps to greatness. Know that you must first get above water before you start shooting for the moon. This takes a combination of both *patience* and *persistence*.

TAKE OWNERSHIP

At the end of the day, this chapter is more a plea for you to take ownership of your life than a revelation of profundity. You can define it however you like, but the bottom line is this: life contains cycles. It is a series of ups and downs, ebbs and flows, good times and bad times. Along with the highs and lows come all the space in between. The importance in this is that we *see it*.

See the beauty of it, the pain in it, the effort expended throughout it, the times of defeat that can't be escaped in the midst of it, and the moments of victory that come after it. See the good it can be used for, be warned of the dangers that are present within it, and recognize that you're a co-passenger on this ride, alongside every other person on this planet.

Anything can be conceptualized with enough time and thought, but the proper application of a concept comes down to you and the daily decisions you make, from the time you wake up to the time you fall asleep. That is truly where the rubber meets the road: "the point at which a theory or idea is put to a practical test."

Momentum can be on your side if you choose it to be. Make it your teammate or it will forever work as your enemy.

You decide.

FAILURE

"Failure is not the opposite of success, it's a stepping stone to success."
—ARIANNA HUFFINGTON'S MOTHER

MY STORY

If you haven't noticed, there's one common thread that each illustration from my life shares. It is the most pervasive theme throughout much of my life and one of the greatest growth stimulants I know. This thread is none other than *failure*.

Failure was one of the biggest motivating factors in my golf career. It was a driving force that propelled my relentless pursuit of excellence. But above and beyond golf, failure was the tutor that gave me both the content and the desire to write this book. This book that you're now reading can in many ways be attributed to failure.

PROFESSIONAL GOLF

I find it very fitting for me to be writing this chapter at the conclusion of my golf career. If a post-career analysis was done on the results of my time as a professional golfer, the summary would appear bleak and grim. The cold, objective reality of statistical analysis is that success will only be determined by numbers, the results that were produced. From that perspective, I produced three of the worst years possible in any career path. Minimal improvement in scoring average, slow development in game refinement, lackluster finishes minus a few outliers, and very little monetary return to speak of. Praise God that isn't the full story.

Oftentimes, facts take priority in determining what transpired and how to evaluate it. But facts never tell the full story, and rarely are they adequate in understanding the true merit of what really happened. To say that the past three years were a failure confuses results with reality.

I began professional golf with one mission in mind: to use my God-given and personally refined ability as a golfer, combined with the investment of sponsors, to produce a sustainable and successful career. I understood the challenge that lay before me, but I also knew that a deep understanding would only come by experiencing it personally. With the average time for professional golfers to reach the PGA Tour resting between 7 and 10 years, the road would undoubtedly be arduous. Initially, I committed to three years of playing professionally before reevaluating my career path with my team, to determine the future for this pursuit.

In being committed and sold-out to this path, I didn't allow myself to entertain thoughts of what it would be like to move on, to make the decision to leave the pursuit I worked my whole life to accomplish, to fall into the pool of the majority and *not* become a successful, professional golfer. This reality had never entered into my headspace for any prolonged duration of time.

Then came the three-year mark.

Suddenly, I found myself sitting on the precipice of a career-defining point. Either my career would be defined as in process or a failure. The biggest fear I had always faced is the fear of not being good enough, the fear of not accomplishing what I set out to do, the fear of not living up to expectations, the fear of not performing to the level of my ability—the fear of *failing*. And now, on this precipice of career uncertainty, I was standing face to face with my worst fear.

WHAT FAILURE GAVE ME

I don't want to negate the difficulty of this decision, but I dramatize the narrative in order to highlight the challenge failure provides. In my three-plus years of playing professional golf, failure was a common experience—from day-to-day practice where I would fail to complete certain drills I created, to tournaments where I underperformed either as a whole or in an individual round, and even to rounds of golf played with family and friends when I failed to play how I expected myself to.

With all my efforts focused on succeeding in golf, there was no stone that I was willing to leave unturned. If there was something standing in my way, then I would find a way around it, over it, or *through* it—yet failure was a sizable obstacle, to say the least.

But as experience added up, I began to have a better understanding of it and a better ability to overcome it. The key is intention. With the habits I cultivated as I progressed through my career, I began to grow more and more familiar with both failure and what precedes it. As I grew to understand what factors led to underperforming, I began to recognize the moments when these tendencies would occur in real time. This allowed me to begin working on building the right habits to replace the wrong ones and to start laying the foundation for removing failure's bondage.

This is one of, if not *the,* greatest gifts that professional golf has given me: *the freedom from failure.* Note that this is not the freedom from *failing,* but rather the freedom from what failure often produces: aversion, conservation, timidity, self-deprecation, self-devaluation, and ultimately *fear.* So much of fear is based on unknowns that produce a state of discomfort. The gift of this season in my life, among other things, was gaining a comfort around failure. This comfort is what enables me to act in a way that's unaffected by failure's presence or by the possibility of its future occurrence.

In no way do I want to praise failure as the pearl of highest worth, and I am a big believer in pursuing the endeavors that *bear fruit*—meaning, they produce positive results. What I do hope to share is what golf has given me (and everyone else who plays the game long enough and well enough): a new understanding of failure—and not just a new understanding but also a *rebranding.*

CONCEPT

"No one ever drowned by falling in the water.
They drowned by staying there."
—Steve Sims

A POWERFUL FORCE AT PLAY

North America is a distinct culture but not all that unique. In the "land of opportunity," we have successfully deified success, solidifying our reputation as being an achievement-based culture. Self-worth is defined by self-made success, even though success is never solely made by one's self. In the age of social interconnectedness, portraying the spotless image of you with your best foot forward at all times is the key to living up to achievement's expectations. The possibility is endless; the potential is within; the success is there to be grasped; achievement shall be praised above all else.

One of the concepts we learn about in "Economics 101" is the inextricable link between supply and demand. When supply is reduced, demand will rise, and vice versa. Thus, a high demand infers a low supply. When we transfer this logic to our culture of achievement in America, it is plain to see that success, especially as defined by the world and our culture, is rarely achieved.

With being so connected to so many people, more than ever before, we see images of "success" portrayed more rapidly and more frequently. This leads us to believe that success is normative, and thus, if we don't achieve the success displayed by the people we (virtually) follow and observe, then we are the ones missing out—the minority. But, hey, if you can't walk the walk you might as well talk the talk and portray the image of success for all to see. Really, you're just falling in line with the rest of America.

The term "rat race" is now found in most dictionaries. It's defined as "any exhausting, unremitting, and usually competitive activity or routine, especially a pressured urban working life spent trying to get ahead with little time left for leisure, contemplation, etc." Welcome to America, the country filled with racing rats.

What is the opposite of success? What happens if you don't/can't live the culturally prescribed life of achievement? The result is a seven-letter F-word—a word that is outwardly shunned but inwardly experienced by the masses: *failure*.

This is the story our culture wants us to believe. Success is good: failure is bad. If you succeed, you are worthy of praise. If you fail, you are worthless. Culture's power and influence over us are far greater than we would like to admit. The question is, will you adopt the story or rewrite it?

EXCAVATION

This observation deserves a moment of silence—of pause and reflection.

Because, really, what is success without failure? What is the good without the bad? What is right without wrong? Objectivity would be lost if there was no standard.

So, what is failure exactly?

The most basic observation reveals that failure is a natural and necessary part of life.

Why?

Because we are humans—flawed, imperfect, and in a perpetual struggle. This is a part of what it means to be alive. Ultimately, failure cannot be avoided. It is both a *pervasive* and a *permanent* fixture of life on Earth.

Is it important?

Yes!

(The third why is always the most revealing question of all...)

So, *why* is it important?

Failure is what teaches us right from wrong; it clarifies what is good and shows us where we need help or extra effort.

So here are the questions we must *personally* answer:

- Is failure your friend or foe?
- Your teacher or your assailant?
- Is it helpful or hurtful?
- Do you recognize it or ignore it?
- Do you value it or reject it?

GIVING BIRTH TO FAILURE'S BONDAGE

Failure is a part of life that every human being experiences, but when does it first start appearing? I would argue that we first experience failure when we begin learning how (or attempting) to walk. The interesting part of this early occurrence of failure is that it's *not* ostracized but rather welcomed and encouraged. It is rightly seen as an attempt to improve the quality of our life, opening the door of possibility beyond what can be accomplished from a life spent crawling on all fours.

Throughout most of our early years, we learn to embrace failure as our friend, an aid on the path of learning and discovery. Through failure we learn how to do things correctly and eventually accomplish what we set out to do. In those early years, loving mothers will gently prod their child along the path of failure with detached interest, giving the child the space needed to figure things out while providing helpful bits and pieces along the way.

But at a certain point, things changed.

When we enter the education system, we begin our indoctrination under the achievement culture's gospel. The goals set before us change our approach from learning forward to achieving forward. Priorities shift and grades take control of the throne as the prescribed educational goal to pursue. Unless parents are proactive, this will be reinforced by the praising of achievement instead of effort; and as a child, we quickly learn that the key to achievement is getting good grades, no matter the cost.

As this mindset is transcribed across life, we become enslaved to the bondage of achievement and the fear of failure. Instead of being our ally, failure turns into a dreaded enemy that's tirelessly working toward our demise.

FAILURE'S TRUE PURPOSE

If failure is an inherent part of the human experience, then we must discover its ultimate purpose, as well as it's usefulness in life. It's easy to recognize failure's pervasive and permanent presence in our experience of life; the challenging part is to understand why.

As a Christian, I believe failure is a result of humanity's sin nature. On a cosmic level, it is inextricably tied to our fallenness, and it serves as a never-ending reminder of our need for God. Failure helps us understand our inability to save ourself, ushering in the necessity of redemption—a way to overcome our inability. In light of eternity, that way of redemption is through Jesus Christ. (For more on His story, read the book of John in the Bible.)

Yet, even from an earthly view, failure instructs us on the difference between right and wrong, good and bad, where we are and where we want to be. It is a necessary part of gaining objectivity. And this objectivity is what directs us on the path of improvement, showing us what we need to work on and how to get there.

But failure's true weight in gold is found in its role as the CMO—the Chief Motivation Officer. That's right, the chief motivator in all of life. Without failure, human progress would be nonexistent. Progress itself means that we aren't where we used to be. And the only way we move past our current limitations is by failing enough to learn what *not* to do in order to learn what we need to do to reach the goal set before us. This is true not only on an individual level but also equally on a societal level.

Scarcity is the preeminent feature of anything that's in high demand. Without failure, success would not have the appeal it garners in real life. Failure's prevalence provides the scarcity required for success to be valued, for it to have worth—creating both its demand and its appeal.

The bottom line is this: failure is a powerful part of life and an incredible ally that provides tremendous assistance if viewed properly.

From Thomas Edison: "I have not failed, I've just found 10,000 ways that won't work."

… to Michael Jordan: "I can accept failure, but I cannot accept not trying."

… to Winston Churchill: "Success is not final, failure is not fatal: it is the courage to continue that counts."

… to Henry Ford: "The only real mistake is the one from which we learn nothing."

They saw failure in its true light and lived lives capitalizing on failure's powers. Why aren't you?

WHY WE SEE IT AS BAD

If we're honest with ourself, more often than not we see failure as *the enemy*—and not just an adversary, but the one part of life to avoid at all costs. This mindset is developed in many ways, but at its core is the war for self-worth. When we place our self-worth in our ability to succeed, then failure becomes our greatest fear.

The word that encapsulates self-worth is *identity*. We must place our identity in things that last, on a sturdy foundation that will weather the storms of life. When our identity is found in the results we produce, then our self-worth will be directly tied to success or failure. Since failure can't be avoided, we either fall into a pit of negative self-worth or into a pattern of ignorance. By ignoring the failures, we protect our identity and maintain a positive self-worth; but ignorance never produces change, and without change there cannot be freedom. Both ignorance and self-loathing are losing strategies.

One of the primary times this mindset is developed is during childhood. What begins when we are working hard in school to get good grades can last all the way to our resignation from life in old age. Not only is it formed early, but also it's often reinforced at every step along the way—from elementary school through high school, to college and beyond, into the workforce and climbing the corporate ladder. At any and every stage, success is rewarded and praised publicly, while failure is subsequently devalued and punished. All the honor is given to results, at the expense of process—the how of the success that was created.

This vicious cycle deepens our internal fear of failure until we can no longer produce change in any area of life, leaving us with the feeling that we're helplessly destined to fulfill the role life gives, to simply play the cards we are dealt. As I already mentioned, individuals aren't the primary culprits to blame for this entrapment. The prevailing culture of the Western world is based entirely (and ruthlessly) on achievement, implanting deep in our minds the culture's accepted version of what failure indicates. Parents also play a much bigger role than they know in this cycle.

Dr. Carol Dweck, a psychologist at Stanford University, did a study with four hundred fifth-graders in New York. The study's goal was to determine what effect a single sentence of praise had on performance and effort. Half of the students were praised for their intelligence and half were praised for their effort. Guess which half did better in the long run?

As Daniel Coyle points out in *The Talent Code*, after visiting many of the "talent hotbeds" throughout the world, he affirmed Dweck's findings in saying, "[E]ach of the hotbeds I visited used language that affirmed the value of effort and slow progress rather than innate talent or intelligence" (*The Talent Code*, p. 136). Praising children for their efforts instead of their results will help free them from the future bondage failure brings.

The habits formed during the foundational years of our youth will carry on for the rest of our lives, unless we are able to consciously direct them elsewhere. First impressions are the most important, because the precedent set in the beginning takes much greater effort to change at any point after. The longer you've lived in subjection to failure's bondage, the fiercer the battle will be to regain the lost ground.

But we must know and trust that the fight is worth it!

WHY WE SHOULD SEE IT AS GOOD

While it may be easy for us to agree with the *concept* of failure as something good, it's much harder for us to *believe* that maintaining this perspective is worth the fight. My goal is to provide enough ammunition so that you can finally choose to step into this battle on your own. Because, guess what? Failure isn't going anywhere. It's up to you to decide what you're going to do with it.

And that's the first reason we should see it as good: because it is *inescapable*. So stop running from it! Running from an inescapable reality only produces exhaustion, defeat, and despair. Instead of running from that which you can't outrun—stop! Approach it, get to know it, and embrace it as your friend. It's always uncomfortable and challenging to win over an enemy into a friend, but that doesn't mean it's not worth the squirminess.

Furthermore, we should see failure as good because it *is* good. True joy and beauty are found in the *struggle*, that process of learning that happens most effectively through failing. Why is it the sun shines brightest after a storm? It's the contrast brought by the darkness that makes the light shine brightest. This is also why failure is life's greatest teacher and our greatest ally. We may not like everything that our teacher makes us do, but that doesn't change the purpose behind why they do it: to make us better, smarter, and stronger. The toil in life is what produces the steadfast endurance needed to weather the trials and failures inevitably experienced in life—*that* is where the beauty in life is made to shine brightly.

One of the best byproducts of failure is *humility*. The more we fail, the more we realize we aren't as "special" as we like to think. Failure is the daily multivitamin we must take to remain grounded and humble. It is the reminder that keeps us from becoming a god in our own eyes and returns us to the level field of humanity. This is what enables *empathy*. Empathy is our ability to share in the feelings and experiences of others. When we elevate ourselves above other people (and above our own reality), we lose our ability to meet others where they are and, simultaneously, our ability to accurately see where we are.

Beyond the pain and the struggle, failure is inextricably tied to *joy*. Without failure we would never experience the joy found in triumph, the elation that comes in conquering. What is joy without sorrow?

Failure is life's great clarifier and our marquee motivator. It shows us what's important and reveals what our priorities should be. Ultimately, the more you fail, the more you *can* succeed. Michael Jordan said it best: "I've missed more than 9,000 shots in my career. I've lost almost 300 games. Twenty six times I've been trusted to take the game-winning shot and missed. I've failed over and over and over again in my life. And that is why I succeed."

Failure is the compass needed for life. It's the trusty guide we must look to, as our ally, companion, and friend in the journey we are on. When we don't reach the level of our aspirations, we arrive at the crossroads between our ideals and our reality. The key is to keep both roads in mind, living in pursuit of our ideals while operating in light of reality. This is the space between, the grey zone between who we are now and who we want to be in the future. This is the tension that cannot be avoided, the struggle that can't be skipped.

The struggle is real—but, man, is it good.

APPLICATION

> *"Failure isn't fatal, but failure to change might be."*
> —John Wooden

THE ROCKY ROAD OF APPLICATION

Learning from failing isn't always smooth sailing. It isn't a pleasant walk in the park. And it definitely doesn't disappear.

In January 2016, I slipped off of a rail on my snowboard, falling flat on the cold steel of the round bar that the board was supposed to be sliding on. The direct impact of the bar came on my right abdominal wall, kicking off a chain of events that would last longer than I could have ever imagined. It was the first domino to fall in a string of injuries that would ensue. The advice I had often heard was that "rails aren't worth the risk." Being a competitor, this advice didn't sit well with me, and it took several years of battling the injuries that resulted from *not* heeding those words for me to finally consent to their truth. It doesn't always work this way, and I wouldn't go back and change what happened because of all the fruit it produced, but the truth still remains: *we learn the most through failure.*

The second major battle with injury came in July 2016 in the form of a perfect storm of events: too much time in a car, too little sleep and recovery, too much golf paired with too much anxiety and stress—all leaving my body in a weak and compromised state. When load was added (the golf swing), what resulted was a strained left rhomboid, directly tied to the motion of making a golf swing. Since it occurred in the middle of the busiest portion of my golf schedule, it meant withdrawing from numerous tournaments I had already committed to play in. Muscle strains can be some of the worst injuries because of how deceptive they tend to be; you may think you are close to being healed but in reality there could still be several more weeks (or months) needed to fully recover. Patience is a premium in these times, and patience is exactly what I failed to maintain. Instead of healing in the usual 6 to 8 weeks that most strains take, it took me four months. *Learning from failure.*

But even after four months, the rhomboid injury continued to persist, off and on, for the next 6 to 7 months. During this time I learned *a lot* about the body and gained a much higher awareness of it too. After having little to no success in overcoming the nagging strain, it became apparent that the injury we had been treating was not the root cause. This led to further reflection, brainstorming, and experimentation—all of which pointed to the original snowboarding accident. The trauma from the forceful impact with the rail shut down the neurological connection to that specific area in my body, which in turn led to other parts of my body having to compensate to pick up the slack from the deactivated muscles. The left rhomboid we had been treating all along was merely a symptom, not the root. *Learning from failure.*

I share these examples to help highlight the reality that failing is never glamorous. It won't be fun or easy, but that doesn't alter its benefit. What could I have done differently? How could I have avoided all the problems in the first place? Both of these questions are important to ask, but they can easily miss the point. Our goal should *not* be to never make another mistake or failure again. Rather, it should be to never make the *same* failure again. Repeated failure is often an indicator of ignorance.

Don't waste your failures. Learn from them, and do the work needed to not repeat them.

WHAT KEEPS US IN BONDAGE

As you can see from my own story, many of us are living in bondage to the fear of failure. This is not a place we want to remain, especially when we begin to see the compounding nature of this fear if left unchecked and uncontrolled. In chapter 5, we saw that fear is often based on what others think of us. With the fear of failure, this is almost entirely the case. The longer we remain in this state, the deeper it is planted and the wider it spreads.

A big part of the problem comes from our overemphasis on the *results* at the expense of the *process*. James Clear said it best in that "goals are good for *planning* your progress and systems are good for actually *making* progress." He goes on to refine this further, saying, "Goals can provide direction and even push you forward in the short-term, but eventually a well-designed system will always win. Having a system is what matters. Committing to the process is what makes the difference." We will never gain victory over our fear of failure without shifting our focus from results to processes.

One of the most sinister (and addictive) weapons used by failure's fear is self-limiting beliefs. The narrative we tell ourselves becomes the reality we soon experience. The more we encourage and affirm our inability, the more we will experience and see this reality firsthand. And who doesn't love some good self-deprecation?

This is such a massive issue. When we honestly reflect, we all share in the experience of insulting our own ability and know it makes us feel right at home. But why? In making light of our inability and emphasizing our failure, we outwardly deface its power to those around us, robbing them of the ability to bring us down because we've already beaten them to it. This allows us the easy path of accepting the defeat we are inevitably bound to, and it keeps us from having to own up to the results we desperately want to disassociate with. And since everyone else is doing the same thing, why change?

This speaks to another component of the shackles we live in: the power of the majority. Letting culture (and the prescriptions of those around you) tell you right from wrong is a recipe for self-deception, and it feeds fear of failure the juicy meat needed to keep it alive and well. It is undoubtedly hard to swim upstream, against the tide. Part of that challenge is from the view we have of others' lives. When all we see from everyone else are the success stories, the best days, the most memorable moments, the perfectly planned portraits, then we begin to believe we are alone in this daily encounter with failure. Curated lives have overtaken real lives, and this keeps us from owning up to the current reality in our own life and the failures we can't ignore.

Building further on this, when we succumb to the cultural pressure of curation, we ascribe to the tunnel-vision approach. Since everyone else is living this way, then there is simply no other route to take. This is a classic example of close-mindedness, and living in this ignorance will only strengthen the bond that failure's fear has on you.

The longer we live in this manner, the more internal resistance we will face in changing our ways. This refers back to the "consistency bias" given in *Influence: The Psychology of Persuasion* by Robert Cialidini. The deck is becoming more and more stacked against you. How much (and how long) do you want to fight?

If we want to get to the heart of the matter, self-deception is a *lie*. A lie is something that is false, or *not* true. It is believing in a false reality, and in this case, a self-created false reality. What is the lie of failure's fear? That failure is a waste instead of an *opportunity*. This is *your* choice. Seriously, you get to choose.

But that doesn't make it easy.

HOW TO VIEW IT AS GOOD

There are some ways to make it easier, to help you help yourself. But before we get to the tools, we first need to look at the steps.

Steps are useful in helping us see the process forward as attainable and achievable. Initially, there are only two steps to be taken: (1) see it, and (2) stop it. Seeing it means we take the time and effort to pause what we are doing and recognize the lie for what it is. Failure is *not* a waste but rather an opportunity to learn, grow, and move forward stronger. Stopping it means we simply stop believing the lie to be true. We call it by its true identity, refusing to accept the message it proclaims.

Since the greatest limiting factor in failure is our fear of it, the process involved in overcoming is the same that's used in conquering any fear (as mentioned in chapter 5). It is a five-step process that involves (1) recognition, (2) discovery, (3) replacement, (4) reprogramming, and (5) repetition. (Revisit chapter 5 if you need a further refresher.)

Beyond the process (the steps), there are many ideas, approaches, and tools we can use to gain leverage against our own misconceptions of failure.

- *Make it a lifestyle*—To fully embrace a habit, we must adopt it as our lifestyle. Being healthy isn't a diet; it's a lifestyle. Embracing failure is never contained by a single element but rather a holistic, all-encompassing approach that characterizes our lives.

- *Instill proper systems*—Processes must be in place for us to benefit from our failures. A failure that doesn't produce learning (or change) is a failure *wasted*. And as Henry Ford stated, the only true failure is failing to learn from our failures.

- *Begin living by faith*—Walking by faith means that we are doing something in light of a future hope. It is living for something that isn't fully seen. As a Christian, this is what defines me. But, beyond what we believe about life and death, we can practice walking by faith through the pursuit of lofty goals. The more we pursue challenging endeavors, the more faith we must have that our efforts in the process will produce the desired goal, after a period of committed time.

- *Surround yourself with the same*—You are the sum of the five people you spend the most time with. This cliche is true because of the power of who we interact with most on a daily basis. If we want to conquer failure's fear and begin using failure as an ally, then we must seek out others who are pursuing failure in the same way. This is one of the most practical ways to help ourselves. Curate your own majority.

- *Learn from others' failures*—The more we read or listen to the failures of others, the better we will understand its universality. Even though the fact that failure is shared by every human is undeniable, we still need help believing it. Seek out the stories of failure used well.

- *Create accountability*—One form of accountability would be to have other people literally checking in on you to see if you are consistently embracing failure. But the easier option is to simply *speak openly* about your failures. This is *not* an encouragement to participate in further self-deprecation but rather to communicate what you are *learning* from your failures—which empowers your response and stimulates others to follow suit.

- *Dare to live* —"If the unexamined life was not worth living, was the unlived life worth examining?" (Paul Kalanithi). We must dare to live boldly, accepting the inevitable failures that will come our way, seeing them as the building blocks that create the person we want to be. Dare to live courageously, and watch failure join your team.

- *Recognize your options*—One of the lies that failure's fear likes to tell us is that once you go down a road, there's no return. And if there is a return, it's going to be a long, slow backtrack to point

A before you can begin moving anywhere else. Both of these lies hide the option of a **pivot**. Pivots allow us to capitalize on all the ground we've gained thus far and use it for another pursuit if we fail to reach our initial goal.

- *Baby steps to greatness*—Take it slow, one step at a time. It isn't a single sprint. It's a marathon (which may contain a series of sprints). Be patient.

- *Celebrate your success*—Emphasizing our response to failure has been done at the expense of our successes. Success is a very important part of the journey, and the tendency of us "failure friends" is to move past successes without ever pausing to engage, recognize, and respond to the victory we've just won. We *must* take time to properly celebrate our successes before returning to the battles that lie ahead.

THE DARK SIDE

The problem with the pendulum is that it always swings up on the far side, moving away from being in balance before returning back to the middle. Too often in our attempts to regain balance, we end up overcorrecting. We must always be observant of how far we swing from one side of the pendulum to the other, and then work to find the proper balance of what is optimal.

Here are three ways we tend to overcorrect in transforming failure into our friend and ally:

1. *Not learning from failure*—While this has been mentioned before, it deserves to be re-mentioned. This is *the* failure that turns any failure into a complete waste, a missed opportunity, the one that got away.

2. *Adopting failure as our own*—When we start seeing our failures as intrinsically tied to our inner being, seeing it as our own naturally given character trait, then we reduce our self-worth to that which is below the rest of humanity. Failure is not a person-specific part of life; it is universally shared by all. Disassociate it from your character and release yourself from its power.

3. *Using the good to justify the bad*—When we begin to use the good of failure to inwardly justify its prolonged presence in our lives, then we have swung too far away on the pendulum. The other word for this is *excuses*—passing the blame. Ultimately, this is a failure to take ownership that results in settling for the forever state of failure. Failing is *never* a place to remain in. Stop giving yourself a way out, take ownership, and start seeking success.

Glorification of failure is never the answer. In Peter Brown's book on how to learn effectively, *Make It Stick*, he summarized this best: "It's not the failure that's desirable, it's the dauntless effort despite the risks, the discovery of what works and what doesn't that sometimes only failure can reveal. It's trusting that trying to solve a puzzle serves us better than being spoon-fed the solution, even if we fall short in our first attempts at an answer."

THE END OF THE MATTER

When all is said and done, your response to failure is simply that: up to you. Much has been said about the helpful versus the hurtful perspectives we carry regarding our failures, but the fruit comes from what you do with it.

One final aspect to mention is *regret*. Living with regrets is almost always a result of inaction. Don't let the fear of failure keep you from moving forward. Taking action is what we want to foster in removing the fear of failure. Living life with no regrets is this concept stated in the negative. From the positive or affirmative side, there are two calls to action; and if you leave this chapter with nothing else, let it be these two life mottos: (1) **take ownership**, and (2) **never settle**.

Taking ownership means that we recognize our failures, see them as they truly are, and then use them as they are designed to be used: as a reminder, teacher, motivator, clarifier, humbler, unifier, and trainer. It is our responsibility and goal to take ownership of our failures, allowing us to use them for good and embrace them as our teammate in the path toward our highest potential and our greatest good.

Beyond ownership, we must ensure that we *never* allow ourselves to accept failure as our final destination. Never settling means that we refuse to allow ourselves the easy way out—the path of ignoring, denying, excusing, or refusing the reality of failure. We must never settle for failure but always remain adamant on moving past our current failure and toward that which lies ahead—both successes and failures.

The apostle Paul is one of the most inspirational and powerful men in the Bible. In the book of Philippians, he makes a similar plea to himself and to all the recipients of his letter: "Not that I have already obtained this or am already perfect, but I press on to make it my own, because Christ Jesus has made me his own. Brothers, I do not consider that I have made it my own. But one thing I do: forgetting what lies behind and straining forward to what lies ahead, I press on toward the goal for the prize of the upward call of God in Christ Jesus" (Philippians 3:12-14).

PERSPECTIVE (WHAT NOW?)

"There are, it seems, two muses: the Muse of Inspiration, who gives us inarticulate visions and desires, and the Muse of Realization, who returns again and again to say 'It is yet more difficult than you thought.' This is the muse of form. It may be then that form serves us best when it works as an obstruction, to baffle us and deflect our intended course. It may be that when we no longer know what to do, we have come to our real work and when we no longer know which way to go, we have begun our real journey. The mind that is not baffled is not employed. The impeded stream is the one that sings."

—WENDELL BERRY

NOT KNOWING IS KNOWING

Stated in a shorter and more succinct way:

> *"There will come a time when you believe everything is finished. That will be the beginning."*
> —Louis L'Amour

Stated in a more ethereal and artistic way:

> *"Between the idea / and the reality /*
> *between the motion / and the act /*
> *Falls the Shadow."*
> —T.S. Elliot

I love these quotes because they highlight the inherent tension we face in life. Viktor Frankl stated this well by saying, "Mental health is based on a certain degree of tension, the tension between what one has already achieved and what one still ought to accomplish, or the gap between what one is and what one should become."

Tension is present everywhere. Often, not knowing is the best place to be, even though it is equally the most uncomfortable place to be. Transitioning well in life is all about embracing that tension, the tension of leaving behind where you've been while leaning into the future unknowns of where you're going, and carrying forward the lessons life has brought. There must be a direction for your new path, but the final destination is rarely clear. But it's important to know that clarity isn't what's important—*persistence* is. And not just persistence, but also maintaining curiosity paired with discipline, which will largely determine how successful you are.

In saying "not knowing is knowing," the point is that usually when you reach a place of not knowing, you've reached the limitations of your past experience and are beginning to tread into new waters. This newness allows you to see with child-like eyes, seeing with full comprehension. The problem is, that full comprehension is limited to the immediate vision in front of us, not the future vision of what's to come. This is the place where faith is needed—not only faith, not only in the spiritual sense of trusting in a divine and sovereign ruler who reigns above you, but also faith in the day-to-day grind of life. This is the faith that the efforts you are putting in each day will produce future reward—the fruit of your labor.

PERSPECTIVES

Perspective is an element present in every moment at every stage in life. Simply defined, perspective is how we view the world, how we process the information and events we experience in everyday life. With the vastness of human experience, perspectives can differ greatly. Yet, even in our own experience of life, our personal perspective can have multiple dimensions, and usually it's more subjective than not.

In order to self-correct we must first be self-aware enough to know what needs correcting. Self-awareness entails an objective view of how we personally think and operate, which leads to a greater empathy and understanding toward others with whom our views and perspectives differ.

Perspective is as powerful as it is inescapable. In order to use its power for good, we must be able to see it at play. The three main realms we experience perspective in are (1) the past, (2) the present, and (3) the future. To close out this book's journey from here to there, I want to share some perspectives from the three realms in which I see it now.

PAST (A LOOK BACK)

In looking back at the concepts given in this book, there is value in recalling and remembering.

We must see the path and then commit to it. We must learn how to learn, but then learn how to be taught and who to be taught from. We must see fear for its intended purpose and deface its harmful effect. We must learn systems and then learn about ourselves so that we can learn the best systems for ourself. We must gain awareness of momentum's presence in life and then start using the rhythms of life to our advantage. And we must see failure as friend, not foe, for the gift it gives us and the lessons we can learn.

A LETTER TO MYSELF

As I look back at my own journey, even through the time in writing this book, it has been its own adventure, going from idea to reality. Along with the personal growth gained from writing, there was also a newfound, practical application of the concepts that I never predicted or expected.

While I didn't know it at the time I began this book, upon writing the conclusion, I now find myself having become not just the subject of the book but also the direct object I've been writing to.

When I began this book project, I was in the middle of a recovery cycle (the fourth one) in my ongoing battle with the recurring injury in my left rhomboid. This period of limbo left me with the perfect opportunity to begin the project I felt called to create: writing a book on the lessons I learned from this journey of professional golf. As the initial idea grew and blossomed, it slowly transformed into less of a book on golf and more of a book on life. More specifically, it grew into a book on how to transition well in life—whether that be transitioning from college to career or from one career to a another career or from a specific role to different role. Life is full of changes, and being able to transition well between the changes is an important skill not often discussed.

The ironic part about this book was that, in reaching the conclusion, I found myself in the middle of the biggest transition of my life: moving from the lifelong pursuit of golf to a new career path and journey. All the work poured into this project to help others would now be applied to my own life in approaching this sizable shift in order to do it *well*—both efficiently and effectively.

WRITING CHANGES READING

They say writing a book changes the way we read books. Until I wrote this book, I didn't understand how that could be.

Not everyone will end up writing a book in their lives. In fact, most people won't, despite many having the desire to. But the gift of writing a book is in how we approach the books we read afterwards. Anne Lamott (prolific writer of over 30 books) affirmed this fact when she said, "Becoming a better writer is going to help you become a better reader, and *that* is the real payoff" (*Bird by Bird*).

The distinguishing factor in whether a book is use*ful* or use*less* is whether or not it leaves a lasting impact. This impact can be either intellectual or experiential—changing either the way we think about the world, or the way we interact with the world we live in. The element that has to be present is some sort of change—a change that has lasting presence. It's all about what we take forward with us.

Before I mention my approach to reading for maximizing its usefulness, I want to highlight the main benefit writing gives for reading. When we begin our foray into the writing world, we begin to see a new perspective for every book we read. We start to understand that a book's presence is no indicator of its validity. The fact that it exists does not guarantee that it's a voice worth listening to. To state it simply: we should approach every book with the author in mind. Each book is a "child" of the author who birthed it, and that book's parent has specific goals and ideas that he/she wants to communicate to the audience who interacts with his/her child. As readers, we should approach books with both *curiosity* and *skepticism*.

Seeing as curiosity and skepticism are diametrically opposed, this is a difficult task. It involves living in the tension of being open to what the author is offering as truth while also evaluating the merit of what they are saying in light of *both* our life experience as well as the author's background and experience (to the degree that we know it). This tension not only helps us see books in a more objective light, but it also forces us to approach the book with a greater degree of intention than we normally would.

HOW I READ BOOKS

There are several ways I have grown as a reader in the past year, and I want to share with you some practical tips or ideas that you can use to improve both your enjoyment in reading and your benefit from reading.

Develop Mental Models
A mental model is really just a catchy phrase to talk about having structure. It is helpful to have structure for the information we consume. When we have a preexisting structure (in our mind), it will be easier for us to categorically group the information we are learning, thereby allowing us to store it away in our memory banks in places that will be easier to pull out when we need to recall what we've learned. In relation to reading, mental models help us read more *efficiently* by recognizing the categorical concept the author is communicating and more *effectively* by growing faster and faster in our recognition of those ideas.

Think in Big Concepts Instead of Sound-bites
This is similar to the idea behind mental models. When we read, it is easy to get sucked into the small picture of what the author is talking about in the specific page, paragraph, or sentence we currently are read-

ing. This is amplified by the fact that we typically read a chapter or two per day, which creates spatial gaps between the individual elements we are reading, removing the broader context from our view. The more we can understand the larger concepts each chapter is communicating, and the broader concept in the main thesis of the book itself, the better we can accurately see the smaller sound-bites and the better we will be in remembering and applying those specific details to our lives.

Create a Personalized Reading System
I am all about systems—repeated practices that produce better results. This is true in reading, but everyone does it a little differently. For me, what I do with every book I read is this:

- I will underline interesting statements, facts, or observations that I didn't know beforehand.

- I will highlight important statements or observations that I want to remember.

- I will underline *and* highlight the information of highest importance/profundity.

- I also bracket paragraphs or sections that communicate a broader but nevertheless, important point.

- I will write comments in the margins with specific prompts on how the author's statement impacted me.

How I review books after completing them has changed several times in the past several years, but the important thing is to have intention surround both how you read the book and how you leave the book. A book is only as good as what you leave it with.

Be a Vocal Reader
This is simply a call to share what we are learning as we learn it. The best way to remember and incorporate what we are reading into everyday life is to engage with other people about it. Discuss it with your friends. Discuss it with your spouse. Discuss it with your neighbor. Heck, discuss it with your dog! Ultimately, the more we can interact with the information we read, the better. And talking about it with others will help

us evaluate its merit more objectively and thoroughly than we could on our own. So start sharing.

Read with Context in Mind

This is so important, but it's something that took me a long time to start implementing. Understanding who the author is and what the context he/she is writing from is essential to accurately receiving what the author is communicating. A book is the product of a human being, and a human being is the product of a life's worth of personal (and cultural) experiences. Not only is the author's context important, but so too is our own context when reading it. We also are bringing a life's worth of experiences and context to any book we read, and that will have an impact on our interpretation of what the author is saying. A general awareness of both these elements will serve us well in best understanding what we are reading.

> "Human intellectual development is a lifelong dialogue between inherited tendencies and our life history."
> —Richard Barnet

Read Both Sides of the Argument

Reading critically takes effort, and it never stops. There's a balance to reading critically. It's the balance between innocent credulity and cynical skepticism. It takes a curiosity paired with a need to be persuaded. As you read what the author is saying, be sure to think about both sides of the argument—both the author's view and the opposing view. This will help you think critically and see the information more objectively. Plus, it requires more effort, which helps solidify what you're learning even more.

Learn When to Put the Book Down

This is something I still have a hard time doing. We have all experienced what it's like to want to simply get through a book so that we can finally move on to the next one. But what if we just stopped and moved on to the next book without finishing the one we're reading now? It seems like we are committing a crime against literature and the "rules of reading" if we succumb to those "selfish desires of laziness." The truth is, when a book's usefulness is achieved, we need to move on. Many times, this will mean we won't finish every book we begin.

We can't (fully) judge a book by its cover, which is why we won't know whether the book is worth reading from front to back until we *actually* start reading it. When we get through a third, or a half, or three-fourths of a book, then we will have a much clearer picture of whether it deserves to be read completely or not. There is an endless supply of books, but there's not an endless supply of our time. Know when it's time to call it quits and move on.

FUTURE (A LOOK FORWARD)

Not only should we look back, but also we should strive to gaze into the future. This gazing should entail a manner of dreaming—of imagining the possibility of years to come, of the life that remains to be lived.

WHAT'S AHEAD

As I look to the future and what will be next, this book has helped me feel confident in paving a new path and doing it successfully. Forcing deep and prolonged concentration into any subject matter will produce real and tangible fruit. Oftentimes, we are unsure of whether or not the content will be directly applicable at the point of completion. This is especially of concern in any project that takes more than a year to finish—like this book. The beauty of this concern is seen in its primary flaw: the belief that we know what will be best for ourself in a year's time. When we look to the future, the fact that it is unknown is what creates the novelty, the excitement, and the unending curiosity regarding what's to come.

The danger in pairing novelty with long-term payoff comes from the inevitable distractions along the way. Being committed to a singular pursuit is a challenging endeavor when the road is long. The most common distractions we will face will usually present some form of short-term gain. Delayed gratification takes discipline, but it also takes *persistence*. We must know and trust that the profit will come, whether it be in financial gain or in skills acquired. The payoff will always come, in part, from the experience we gain—the experience of pursuing a lofty goal and pushing ourselves past our conceived abilities and into the realm of *possibility*.

Three quotes really speak to this concept collectively:

"Persistence is the single biggest predictor of future success. And the second thing is curiosity—what do you care about. The combination of persistence and curiosity is a very good predictor of ... success."
—Eric Schmidt

Persistence paired with curiosity is a deadly combination—in the best possible way.

"You'll learn more from the process of pursuing excellence than from the products of achieving it."
—James Clear

The process is where the real value is, especially in terms of personal growth.

"Failure after long perseverance is much grander than never to have a striving good enough to be called a failure."
—George Elliot

So even if our persistence ends in a so-called "failure," or a very real failure, it is still valuable. And as we learned in the last chapter, failure itself is not an enemy to be feared but a friend to embrace and an ally to partner with.

HOW TO DREAM

One of my favorite things to do is dream—but not while I'm sleeping. Daydreaming is frowned on by some, but I believe in its power, and so should you.

In fact, dreaming seems like one of the easiest ways to reconnect with our childhood self. In the younger years of our life, the future is full of *endless* possibility. It is so ambiguous yet so magical—thinking about what the future may be or what we might become. As adults, this would be considered "wishful thinking," or "wasted time," or "an escape from reality/responsibility." These responses can definitely be valid, and many times they are. Daydreaming *can* be all those things; and without a greater "why", they may quickly become them.

For daydreaming to be profitable, the goal cannot be limited to ourself. It must contain an element of benefit for others. And it must be connected to our greater why, the purpose for which we live.

Here are some ways I think about dreaming for the future:

Balancing Present with Future
It is a balance—striving not to err too far on one side or the other. On one side, having future goals and dreams can lead to turning a blind eye to the present, resulting in stagnation. On the other side of the pendulum, having a focus on the present moment can eliminate any thought spent on where we're heading—or where we *actually* want to head.

Using the Subconscious
The subconscious is a powerful force in our lives, and it's a force largely unknown to our conscious mind. The power of daydreaming comes through the work put in by the subconscious. Dreams feed our subconscious with little ideas, nuggets of a concept that are cultivated, unbeknownst to us, over a period of time until it either bears fruit or dies off. In order to give your dreams the best chance of bearing fruit, recognize the subconscious's role and allow space for it to go to work.

Sharing Your Dreams
At a certain point, dreams are meant to be shared. A singular view is never full or complete, and having other people weigh in on our ideas and musings helps broaden our perspective. The biggest help this provides is in opening the door for possibility. The second we communicate what has been isolated in our head, we take the first step toward actualization. Granted, there are many, many more steps to come, but sharing our dreams about the future facilitates a notable shift in how we think about our own dreams.

Seek Diverse Perspectives
Not only should we share our dreams, but also we should share them with a diverse group of people. As we share a dream with a wider pool of people, we will begin to get a clearer understanding of whether or not it is a worthy idea—whether the dream is worth further cultivation or if it should be discarded for other possibilities. Again, a balance must be found in how wide and how deep our diversity pool becomes. Too many people will lead to confusion, and too much diversity will lead to discarding the idea entirely.

Challenging, Not Impossible
There is always a difficulty sweet spot to be found. The hard part about dreaming is knowing what contains a glimmer of hope and what is an inevitable dead end. There are pursuits that seem impossible, and then there are pursuits that are *actually* impossible. Knowing one from the other takes time, but finding the sweet spot should always be kept in mind—because a dream is just that: a future idea that is currently outside of our grasp. To grow, we must strive to take hold of that which is beyond our present reach.

Patient in Pace
It is important to be patient in the pace at which we dream, allocating enough time for the subconscious to process and refine those dreams. Pacing both the excitement and attention we give to each idea is a part of the process that helps refine what is good and what is bad. Small thoughts over a long period of time are usually the recipe for success when it comes to daydreaming. The two places we tend to stumble in this regard are either in becoming overly excited and gung ho or in forgetting or losing sight of the dream in the first place. But really, the second one may not be all that bad if the dream wasn't worth remembering in the first place.

Realistic About the Sacrifice
When dreams begin to surface, creeping closer to our foresight and peaking over the horizon of our future life, this is the time when we must evaluate the sacrifice. Every pursuit contains an opportunity cost—doing one thing means that we can't do countless others. Beyond opportunity costs, dreams are bold, daring, and challenging endeavors. With greater difficulty comes greater sacrifice. We need to see, as objectively as possible, the real sacrifices that are required to turn a dream into a future reality so that we are best prepared for it to actually happen.

At the end of the day, dreaming can be a great thing, and it is a practice we would all do well to embrace. In a podcast interview I did this past year, one of the guests highlighted the importance of possibility. So often we look at the regret and not at the possibility, keeping us stuck in time and unable to act on what our heart truly desires. This is the shift from living in the present to living in the possibilities.

May we all be people who are striving to *live in the possibility*.

PRESENT (THE HERE AND NOW)

Finally, we arrive at *the now*—our present moment in time, when what is to come turns into what is and finally into what was before. There's one last aspect to highlight in looking at the summation of all that's been said. It involves what I consider to be my most important muscle.

MY MOST IMPORTANT MUSCLE

Writing teaches us a lot, not only on how to be a better reader, but also about who we are deep down at our core. It exposes strengths and weaknesses in a new light and creates lasting accountability to live up to the words we are sharing.

When examining the concepts I've shared in this book, there is one foundational element that hasn't been mentioned at length. This observation came to me in discussing the book with my grandfather, who was sharing suggestions and advice for the best path going forward. The character trait that has grown and developed most over the years of playing golf professionally is the one component that has enabled all I currently do and all I will pursue in the future. This element is none other than *discipline*.

In many times and in many ways, mothers can make us blush. One of the ways I have seen my own mother accomplish this is in a surprising comment she's repeated. On numerous occasions, I remember her saying that I am "the most disciplined person" she knows. When I hear this, two responses immediately come to my mind: (1) "You really must not know that many people," and (2) "You obviously don't know me as well as you think you do!" But what these responses reveal is less about my mom's misgivings and more about my own blindness to one of my greatest personal strengths: the discipline of *discipline*.

Much has been written on discipline, both on what it means and how to create it, which is why I don't plan on writing extensively about it here. What I do want to share is an exhortation on why we should strive for a life of discipline.

A helpful way to think about this is to look at the field of creativity, and more specifically at "creation" itself. For anyone to create something, there must be structure for them to create within. For a shape to be a shape, there must be defined borders for it to represent a shape. For computer code to be written, there must be a language it is based off of and a defined screen that it will eventually be displayed on. For art to be art, it must fall within the boundaries of what that art is defined by, even if that definition is itself abstract.

Andy Crouch explains this idea in his book *Culture Making*, where he says, "[C]reativity cannot exist without order—a structure within which creation can happen." Referring to God's creation of the world, he goes on to say that "the Creator's greatest gift to his creation is the gift of structure—not a structure which locks the world, let alone the Creator himself, into eternal mechanical repetition, but a structure which provides freedom" (*Culture Making*, p. 22).

To bring this idea back to discipline, in order for us to create our best work and lean furthest into our own strengths, we must maintain a high level of personal discipline that provides the structure for us to be the best we can be. Discipline trumps motivation; discipline trumps spontaneity; discipline trumps intuition; discipline trumps emotion; and discipline trumps freedom. The reason it trumps all of these other important parts of our life and our work is that discipline is the cornerstone that amplifies all of those other characteristics—bringing out the best version of each piece, making the whole that much richer and that much sweeter.

STRENGTHENING THE MUSCLE

Discipline is a muscle of the mind. Unlike physical strength, mental strength is not seen by weight but by willpower—the determination to do what we know we need to do at the times when we least want to do it.

Here are some practical suggestions on ways to build discipline:

- *Cold showers*—This is one of the least fun but most powerful ways to create discipline daily. There are many physiological benefits to the practice, but the simple truth is that they're never fun. And that's where the gold in its practice is found: the daily opportunity to do something you don't want to do (and something that has no negative effects other than discomfort).

- *Accountability*—Creating discipline is challenging, which is why having teammates to help us grow discipline is ideal. Working out is always more fun with people, and Crossfit is a good example of the power of accountability—both through the community aspect and the financial commitment we make to join. We need others to help us keep the commitments we make—to become mentally strong and disciplined people.

- *Challenging goals*—Again, pushing ourselves past our comfort zone helps highlight the need for discipline in and throughout our lives. Challenging but realistic goals (finding that sweet spot) help us by providing and applying pressure to our abilities. This pressure creates tension and refines our capacities, strengthening them by breaking them down—similar to the process of building physical muscle.

- *Consistency*—"Discipline" is a fancy term to describe mental habits. Habits are when we incorporate an action into our lives and turn it into our default response. This takes consistency over time, and typically that time can take anywhere from 21 to 63 days, depending on what research we follow. Along the way, life will do its best to throw as many wrenches at our newfound goal. Habits need time and effort combined to create consistency. The truth is, disciplines must be fought for if they are to ever be achieved.

- *Working out*—A good way to look at physical exercise and discipline is to see them as siblings. Exercise is a discipline, one of the most beneficial disciplines we can incorporate into our lives. The reason it merits that title is because of how it impacts all other areas. I've discussed this before, but if we want the most bang for our buck in building discipline, then working out will compound benefit into all parts of our lives, including mental discipline.

- *Sleeping well*—Sleep is another compounding force that affects (both positively and negatively) every area of our lives. If we aren't getting the quality and quantity of sleep we need, then discipline will be much harder to achieve.

- *Surrounding ourselves with disciplined people*—Again, the cliche is true: "We are the sum of the five people we spend the most time with." If we want to create discipline, then we need to hang out with disciplined people.

- *Schedules*—This is one of the most practical ways to earn simple discipline gains. Create a schedule daily, weekly, and even monthly—then stick to it.

- *Living with purpose*—Intention is everything. When we live underneath our overarching purpose, we have a reason to develop and commit to being disciplined.

- *Journaling*—This is a great tool for self-evaluation. Spending time, either in the morning or evening, to pause and observe where we are winning and losing the battle is important for consistency in the pursuit of discipline and for improving the quality of our pursuit along the way.

- *Meditation*—This is one of the hardest disciplines to incorporate, but it can be one of the most powerful. The challenge comes in it being counterintuitive. It is stopping in order to move forward better. It is removing thoughts in order to think better. It is an endeavor of fruitlessness, but it can lead to bearing more fruit than ever before. And it is a great discipline of the mind that is worth the sacrifice of time.

- *Self-narrative*—With so much of our self-identity being wrapped up in our perception of ourself, viewing yourself as a disciplined person can be one of the most powerful tools in creating and committing to that discipline.

- *Incentives*—Who doesn't love a good incentive? We can use incentives in many ways to help us in our weaknesses and to grow the discipline needed when we don't know if we have the strength to yet. Incentives are the training wheels for riding the bike of discipline, and they can be a vital part of getting us moving down the path of discipline no matter how young or old we are.

The immature way to think about discipline is to view it as *limiting*. I say "immature" because it is a view of discipline that depicts only the surface level. Beneath the surface, at the heart of discipline, is the key to unlocking our truest and highest level of creativity. We must move past an elementary understanding of discipline and see the true beauty that it brings. Jocko Willink frames it so well: discipline truly does equal freedom.

TO CONCLUDE

This has been a journey from here to there. Now that we're there, where do we go from here?

This book has been a process of its own. Throughout the process, I have gone in one direction only to arrive and then go towards another. And I think that's the point.

When we get to *there*, we must continue onward, moving yet again from here to there.

This is not the start, nor is it the end. It is a new beginning. And what's to come will inevitably be a chance to begin again.

What now? I've done my part, now it's time for you to do yours.

"It's not having the information that's important,
It's what you do with it."
—Bill Keller

AFTERWORD: THE YEAR AFTER

"There are many who seek knowledge for the sake of knowledge: that is curiosity. There are others who desire to know in order that they may be known: that is vanity. Others seek knowledge in order to sell it: that is dishonorable. But there are some who seek knowledge in order to edify others: that is love."

—ST. BERNARD OF CLAIRVAUX

"The bottom line is this: it might be nice to tell yourself that you're going to change, but getting specific makes it real and gives you a reason and a reminder to get back on track whenever you slip up. Soon is not a time and some is not a number."

—JAMES CLEAR

"Now is the magic word of success."

—DAVID SCHWARTZ

IT'S HARD

Writing a book is hard.

The year after beginning this book, and now to seeing it through to completion, has implanted this reality into my being through the school of hard knocks—*experience.*

Ideas are cheap; it's the actions that cost. The true and refined gold is found in turning an idea into reality. And gold is a scarce resource for a reason!

Writing a book is something I wish everyone would do. While it would be a good feat for anyone to accomplish, realistically not everyone can. But if you can, you should.

Regardless of what comes, the fruit of taking an idea and turning it into a tangible product you can hold is worth its weight in experiential gold, no matter what physical gold may result.

Even with that pep talk, recommending that you write a book is cheap; it's easy for me to do standing here typing the words out on my laptop. Here are some simple truths: (1) Writing a book: a great idea! (2) Writing a book: a *very* difficult and challenging endeavor. I wish hearing this simple truth had better prepared me for the obstacles I would face, but I think that wish is an impossible reality.

> *"The most expensive currency in the world is experience."*
> —Whitney Wolfe Herd

The "year after" has been full of the tumultuous ride that's called life. Writing a book has been its own micro-depiction of the highs and lows faced in life—from the early highs of beginning the project, to the early realizations that this was a much bigger task than I had anticipated, to the fierce determination to bulldoze my way through the initial draft, to the disheartening realization that the first draft was crap, to the confusion on how to remedy my lackluster manuscript, to the slow whittling away at the needed improvements, to the final push to refine and perfect all the missing elements needed, to the months of cold emailing and pitching agents and publishers, to the accumulation of rejections and dismissals, to the stagnancy of waiting on someone to finally see the value in my work, to the realization that I had to get better at convincing and incentivizing others of this perspective, to the decision to take ownership and pursue self-publishing, to all the additional tasks to be completed for that route, to finding the funds to invest in an initial run of books, and to finally holding this creation in my hands.

Words cannot do justice to the feelings, thoughts, doubts, uncertainties, unknowns, and frustrations faced in this journey. The year-after is that time after committing to our "grand" idea that is destined for success. It is the time when rubber meets the road, and we travel and travel and travel, farther down the path we committed ourself to, with an increasingly disenchanted view of what we're trying to do.

Writing a book is a good micro-picture of the path to mastery, and both pictures are the illustration of the broader picture of the human experience called life.

REMINDERS

During the year-after, there has been much self-talk—the inner-dialogue between my brain and my emotions, the preaching to myself to keep me on the straight and narrow of the path I committed to.

Here are some of the most common sermons:

1. *Building anything (and everything) takes time—and usually, lots of it.*
   Rome, one of the greatest empires in all of history, was *not* built in a day. In his book titled *Culture Making*, Andy Crouch makes a poignant observation: "The only thing you can do with Rome in a day is burn it." Just as with building a physical home or structure, turning architectural plans into a physical building takes a combination of patience and persistence, working daily to put the pieces together in the proper order to facilitate the final product in the most efficient and effective way possible. The day-to-day view of this requires constant reminders of this reality, and it takes a constant vision that keeps the end goal in sight.

2. *Hearing about it being hard and experiencing the challenges, obstacles, and setbacks are two entirely different things.*
   I wish there was another way around this, but I'm afraid it just takes living it out. What has been helpful is in remembering this reality and reminding myself that I should have expected the very things I'm experiencing: the hardships, setbacks, and difficulties. So while we can't avoid it, we can become faster at reminding and regaining proper perspective on those said realities.

3. *The fruit isn't often found or seen in the moment.*
   Moments provide feelings and experiences and emotions, but rarely do they provide immediate fruit. And if they do, they don't provide the kind of fruit that lasts. In understanding that fruit will not be found in the daily moments of daily work, tasks, and responsibilities, we will be able to overcome the disappointment in not seeing it some days, or even most days.

4. *Insecurities are an effect, not a cause.*
   Meaning: doubts and insecurities will always accompany the human experience, especially when we are pursuing the path of mastery, or putting ourselves out there on any given platform. They should always

remain an effect of what we are producing and not a cause of what we choose to do. We must keep fear from dictating our response, choosing to live proactively and not reactively. This is one of those truths that will be a recurring reminder, especially in writing a book.

5. *Objectivity is never a given.*

Striving to see our work and our path objectively will always take intentional effort. Usually, it takes increasing effort the farther down the road we go. With greater and greater commitment to any endeavor, we face greater and greater internal opposition to seeing our work from a different view or in a different light. The more committed, the more obstinate we become. Seeing with an objective lens is always helpful, and we must strive to remind ourselves that we are always fallible, no matter where we are on the path to mastery.

6. *The learning is in the doing.*

Doing the work set before us is what produces the learning, not the other way around. So many times I've wanted the opposite to be true—for the learning to produce the doing—but the learning doesn't automatically lead to the doing. Doing the work and putting one foot in front of the other is the necessary fuel for learning and the all-important oil for keeping our engines running clean in traveling down the path to mastery.

7. *Challenging things affirm that we are on the right path.*

The fact that the work we are doing is incredibly challenging is evidence supporting the fact that it's worth doing. Nothing worthwhile is ever easy. Something that has worth, that has value to be gained, will always be challenging in some manner or regard. Seeing challenges as proof that we're on a worthwhile track is an important reminder we all could use more often.

THE JOURNEY

"It's not the destination, *it's the adventure along the way."*
—Jake Blauvelt

"The journey is the destination."
—Dan Eldon

"Life is a journey, not a destination."
—Ralph Waldo Emerson

"Success is a journey, not a destination."
—Ben Sweetland

The journey is what makes the destination special, it's what makes the destination worth it.

Imagine running up a hill in your neighborhood. This will be taxing in the moment and physically demanding at times; so when you get to the top of the hill, you may end up pausing to enjoy the view before continuing on with the run.

Now imagine climbing a mountain. After three or four hours of hiking, climbing, trekking up this mountain, you finally reach the summit and all you want to do is stay there and soak in the majesty of the view for as long as possible. You may even spend an hour doing just that!

What if climbing the mountain only took ten minutes of effort? Do you think you would spend an hour soaking it in? Maybe, but far less likely than if you hiked up for three to four hours.

The point is this: the journey is what makes the destination the destination. Without the sacrifice needed to get to the destination, it wouldn't really be a destination.

This perspective is helpful in understanding and valuing the process—in enjoying the journey no matter how long or arduous it may be.

Let's enjoy the ride, because the ride is what makes the destination so special.

HERE VS. THERE

There is never an ultimate "there" in life.

So appreciate your "here" for what it is.

Sometimes, something as simple as a "t" is all you need, to get from here to there.

ACKNOWLEDGMENTS

Writing a book is a massive undertaking. Even with going the self-publishing route, there is always a team of people who end up contributing their efforts, time, expertise, and energy to making the end product what it has become.

I want to thank Dee Moore for the gift of being my early editor. In the beginning of this book, she patiently and lovingly supported my feeble efforts at putting together a string of thoughts that were coherent, and she didn't totally dash all my hopes and dreams (even though she could have with how bad the first draft was!). The early stage of any book is often the most fragile, and it is because of Dee's support and guidance that this book made it to the finish line.

Special thanks are due to my amazing, supportive, and loving family. To my parents, Grant and Becky: your constant support in any and all of my pursuits means the world to me, and this book is no exception. To Jon and Court: your feedback is always so helpful, and much of this book can be attributed to the influence you've both had on my life.

Thanks are also due to Grandpa Peter and Grandma Jan—blessings from God. Peter's wisdom, support, and influence in my life cannot be overstated. He has been a constant voice of guidance over the past five years, and I can't imagine the decisions I would have made without his guidance. Jan is my biggest cheerleader, and her love and encouragement and care are felt deeply and have meant the world to me.

I want to thank my brother and co-host on the podcast, Adam Setser, for his refining and encouraging friendship over these years. There are few friendships that I would consider as rich as ours, and much of this book has stemmed from our partnership in the podcast and the life we have shared over the past seven years.

Thanks are definitely due to the numerous other people who helped influence and shape this book from manuscript to final product: Bill Denzel—your kindness and wisdom were a major influence and help for me in making decisions late in the game; Andy Crouch—having input from your expertise and experience gave me the confidence I needed in making decisions along the way for my first foray into the world of writing; Josiah Zimmerman—your design skills have been on full display over the past few years, and I can't thank you enough for all the awesome work you have done for me, including this killer cover; Nate Neven—having your feedback and edits in the final push to get this manuscript where it needed to be was a gift and blessing to me; Paige Price—having your feedback and suggestions on the best path forward and what pieces to put into place for launch were a major help.

I also want to thank the men who grew my skill and expertise on the links: Jason Semelsberger and John Ray Leary. Coach Jason—your influence on my life helped steer me in the right direction during one of the most pivotal periods of my life: the collegiate years. The systems and disciplines you provided through the team, and the life guidance and influence you gave in the years after, have been both instructive and supportive. Coach JRL—being able to work with you during the professional years grew my game and my understanding of the game in major ways. Having your support and instruction was helpful in navigating the "simplicity on the far side of mastery" stage as a pro, and those lessons fueled the information relayed on these pages as well.

And not to forget the coach who grew my skill and knowledge of the body—Cody Burkhart. Your knowledge (and obsession) with the body and performance helped me grow in my own love and understanding of optimizing performance. You took a chance on me and walked beside me (virtually) through the tumultuous ride that was the last few years of my professional career. Being associated with you and the crew at PSE has been a massive growth factor for my own development, and I'm so grateful to have gained you as a friend/brother along the way.

Last, but first in my heart and most important, I want to thank God for redeeming me through His Son, Jesus Christ, who is my life. All that I do is "from Him, and through Him, and to Him" (Romans 11:36).

RECOMMENDED READING

Make It Stick—Peter Brown

JamesClear.com—James Clear Blog

The Dip—Seth Godin

When Breath Becomes Air—Paul Kalanithi

Fierce Conversations—Susan Scott

About Face—Col. David Hackworth

Influence: The Psychology of Persuasion—Robert Cialdini

The Rise of Superman—Steven Kotler

Deep Survival—Laurence Gomez

The Tipping Point—Malcolm Gladwell

The Seven Habits of Highly Effective People—Stephen Covey

The Talent Code—Daniel Coyle

Bird by Bird—Anne Lamott

Culture Making—Andy Crouch